Praise Fron

Theodora: I think you are amazing. Your writing has had such a positive impact on my view of family life and myself as a mother. I will always be grateful. Keep up the good work.

Nicola: You always hit the nail on the head!

Neil: Liz, oh how this strikes a chord! So refreshing and entertaining.

Andy: Absolutely brilliant, Liz. You tell it like it is, and never fail to uplift.

Nikki: Reading your books is like talking to a friend: you write with gut-wrenching honesty, bravery, compassion, and you connect totally with the reader. Your writing has truth, heart and strength, with loads of cheeky wit too. I can be tear-filled one minute, then laughing like a drain the next. It's just cracking.

Georgia: Brave and inspiring, Liz. It's made me cry!

Chrissie: Your book was great, so many moments where I nodded my head in agreement, and felt that, hey, I'm not the only one who has moments where I feel like I'm doing a terrible job! I'm really looking forward to reading the next book!

Lu: Your books are great. Realistic, funny, and encourage us all to be a bit more tolerant with ourselves. I always recommend them to my friends!

Natasha: Always inspirational!

Jo: I'm greedy to gobble up your next book!

Freddie: So glad it is not just my family that is like that. You make me feel so much better.

Anna: You hit the nail on the head and touch people in a light-hearted way… and that sometimes can make a big difference to someone's day. I know it did mine in the early days of parenthood and later when the rose-tinted specs of family life started to slip. Thank you!

Olga: Thanks for your generosity in sharing all you have learnt and also for your transparency and courage to show us the real you – and the real us.

Sophie: Congrats on the brilliantly helpful, beautiful books!

Eve: Glad you've finished this new book! I've loved your writing since your *Yummy Mummy* book days. (I loved them!) They helped me weather the early stages of being a mummy to a baby and toddler. It's the only book I managed to read since becoming a mum!

Sarah: Loved your first books – and now in my mid-forties I need this one! You are very kindly helping me through this lark they call parenting. Thank you!

Jane: Have been waiting for a book like this to come along for ages. I read your *Yummy Mummy* book when my youngest was little and it really resonated with me: funny, honest and truthful and authentic, you are a writer I can really trust about parenting and all its ups and downs. Now my youngest is nearly eighteen and I'm soon to be fifty, I can't wait to hear your take on this stage of life.

About the Author

Liz Fraser is one of the UK's best-known writers and broadcasters on all aspects of modern family life.

Her books about the realities of being a parent smashed the parenting mould over a decade ago by finally allowing it to be funny, and accepting that we all get most of it wrong – which is just as it should be.

Liz appears frequently on national TV and radio with much bigger hair than she has naturally, on a range of shows including *This Morning*, *Good Morning Britain*, *BBC Breakfast*, Sky News, *5 News* and some local stations nobody listens to and who don't pay.

She has written features for the *Sunday Times*, the *Guardian*, *Grazia*, *Glamour*, *Marie Claire, Red*, the *Daily Mail*, *Mother and Baby*, *Junior*, *Woman*, *Runner's World* and many others, wrote the much-loved 'Three Teens and a Baby' column for the *Telegraph*, and the back-page column 'No, It's Not Just You' in *Essentials* magazine, just before it folded. She takes no responsibility for this.

In 2015 Liz took a sketchy outline of *The Middle Years* to the Edinburgh Fringe for a full run of one-woman stand-up shows, to critical acclaim by three people, at least one of whom was half awake.

Liz has four children, ranging in age from twenty-two (last seen taking money out of her wallet and wearing her shoes) to two (last seen wiping snot on her trousers).

She has a degree in Experimental Psychology and Neuroscience from Cambridge University, and is a passionate mental health campaigner and director of the mental health platform Headcase. She is also an annoyingly competitive 10 km and half-marathon runner – though her knees are no longer very keen on this.

The Middle Years

The Middle Years

WHEN THE KIDS GROW UP... AND
EVERYTHING GOES TITS DOWN

Liz Fraser

This edition first published in 2020

Unbound
6th Floor Mutual House, 70 Conduit Street, London W1S 2GF
www.unbound.com

ISBN (eBook): 9781789650808
ISBN (Paperback): 9781789650792

Cover design by Mecob

Printed and bound in Great Britain by Clays Ltd, Elcograf S.p.A.

To every parent struggling through the Middle Years, and every single one of you who encouraged and supported me to keep going (and going and going and going!) until I finally finished this book.

You know who you are.

Thank you.

Trigger warning:

Some words in this book may cause you to feel something.

You're welcome.

Contents

THE MIDDLE YEARS

That stage of family life when our children selfishly stop being all cute and kissable, and suddenly start sprouting body hair and attitudes, pull away from us and grow taller than us, and even though we were absolutely ASSURED BY EVERYONE that life would get much easier at this point and we would Get Our Life Back – YESSSS!! – that promise turns out to be total horseshit.

It doesn't get easier at all. It just gets differently difficult in more fiendishly, confusingly difficult ways than we could ever have imagined.

Great.

It's a stage when many of us feel a bit lost and confused about who exactly we ARE, now that we've finally emerged like a crumpled, sagging butterfly from the relentless, sleepless tunnel of toddlers and tantrums, so we're not sure exactly which life it is we're supposed to be trying to GET back, even if we could.

It's not an age. It's a STAGE.

Of life.
Of them.
Of us.
Welcome, my friends, to the Middle Years.

Prologue

This is not a book about parenting.

There are 1.3 billion of those already, and most of them make us feel like epic failures in every imaginable way – because that's exactly what parenting feels like.

Instead, this is a book about us. You and me. The knackered, desperate humans, flailing about in the long-awaited Middle Years when our babies have finally grown up, and everything has gone a bit… tits down.

It's the book I wish someone had written for me years ago – it would've saved a *lot* of wrinkles, vodka and therapy bills. Cheers for that.

Because one afternoon, deep in the crusty elbow-skin of midlife family chaos, listening to my teenagers' doors slamming, fielding yet more unpaid bills, sibling civil wars, missed work deadlines and the Incredible Never-Ending Laundry Pile, and realising my sex appeal was now more of a *Blue Peter* crisis fund, I suddenly thought…

Excuse me, but WHAT THE F**K IS THIS??

Why is nothing even *vaguely* as I expected it would be at this stage in my life?

Why did everyone say everything would get easier when my kids kindly sodded off to school, when it actually feels like my life is being set on fire and shoved through a blender every hour before being eaten by a pack of rabid, badly dressed wolves?

Who are these zit incubators loafing about in a cloud of deodorant, Snapchatting each other at dinner and staying up later than me?

Why don't they giggle any more?

Why can't I understand anything they say?

How am I supposed to help with their GCSE maths when I was so staggeringly shit at it the first time around? Is this supposed to be some form of maternal torture?

Why can't anyone else in my house carry things from the bottom of the stairs to the top?

And who keeps nicking my eyeliner?!

Why am I not a self-made millionaire yet, when I've sat through every series of *The Apprentice* since it started, and I even MADE NOTES?

Why am I suddenly scared of lifts? In fact, why am I suddenly cripplingly anxious about loads of things I never had a problem with before?

Why do I cry so much? Why do I get so angry? Why do I get so down, without any warning?

Am I… going *mad*?

Why do I suddenly feel so out of love with the person I spawned the aforementioned zitty Snapchatters with?

Is divorce *really* more painful than knowing Donald Trump exists?

And excuse me, but what the *heck* has happened to the skin above my knees?!

With the glorious, long-awaited and hard-earned freedom that comes with school-age kids, why don't I feel… happier? More confident? More… me?

Who even IS 'me' now?

GUYS, IS ANY OF THIS NORMAL??!

Following a comprehensive rummage through the Rotting Salad Drawer of Midlife Parenting™, I have discovered that all of this is, in fact, entirely normal.

Despite the giant Carrot of Bullshit dangled before our weary eyes during the crippling Early Years of parenting, willing us to Keep Calm And Carry On Bum-Wiping, and promising a heavenly future of nine-hour sleeps, career highs and a return to a social life, our problems don't go away when our children hit school and sign up to limitless free childcare on Instagram; they just become different.

Instead of nappies and broken nights we juggle A-level options and puberty; relationship breakdowns (theirs and our own) and unfathomable sadness; teenage eye-rolls and three-hour queues for the bathroom; career disasters and a creeping, deepening sense of loss as the little people we've been trying to get a break from for fifteen years suddenly start to pull away from us, and we realise that now they're kindly giving us the break we wanted, we actually miss them terribly, and…

… Jesus, is that CHIN HAIR??

Everybody goes through this shit.

IT IS NOT. JUST. YOU.

This, my friend, is golden information. If they could make watches or dental fillings out of it, they would. I can offer neither of these things, but I *can* say:

Come here. Sit down. You are among friends. Despite being a reasonably competent adult, I, too, have eight pairs of pants gathering dust on my bedroom floor, half a kilo of soggy granola in my bag and no idea how to refill the dishwasher's rinse aid thingy without YouTubing it. I can store half a Sunday roast in the gap between my teeth, I still get acne, and I feel confused and sad sometimes. And scared. And a bit lost. And that's all OK.

I wish someone had told me all this.

I also wish someone had told me there are loads of unexpectedly fantastic things about the Middle Years, amid all the stress and chaos: watching our children grow into independent, unique, inspiring adults; career changes we never imagined would happen; achievements we never expected to, erm, achieve; feeling ourselves grow into who we are now, and learning to survive and thrive in a thousand challenging situations we might never have imagined we'd face

– often emerging stronger, and better *humans*, than we were before.

In a way, this isn't really a 'book' at all. Sorry.

It's sort of… a list.

A list of lots of things I wish I'd known before I came to know them – in case it helps anyone else to know them sooner than I did.

(Keep up…)

By the time it's published I'm sure there will be several hundred more things I could have added, that I'll wish I had known at the time I'm writing these words, but annoyingly I have to wait until they've happened to me. I've cried a lot, felt really stupid that I didn't handle it better, and then been all, 'Ohhhhhhhh, I see. NOT like that. Got it.'

Coz life.

This book won't win awards or be lauded as a ground-breaking piece of philosophy that changed the way the world works, improved Humankind, made bees happier or stopped cheap T-shirts from shrinking on their first wash EVEN AT 30 DEGREES.

Some of it's funny. Some is sad.

Some is long.

Some is just in bullet-points because I was in a bullet-pointy mood when I sat down that day, and bullet-points is whatchyer gettin'.

I even threw in a couple of poems-song-things, because life is less shit when you sing it.

There's no beautiful coherence or clever story arc, and it's probably all in the wrong order and missing a few really important points that I urgently scribbled on a piece of tissue paper in a café a few years ago so I'd DEFINITELY NOT FORGET THEM, and now can't find it.

But you know what? It's done, it's honest, and it's for YOU.

If even one of you reads a line or two and feels it speaks to you, it's exactly what you needed to hear right now and it's made your day less 'aaargh', then I'm very happy.

So come! Let's stagger on together and laugh heartily at all the things nothing but surgery and excessive masturbation can cure.

When we're done, come and see me in the pub.

Thank you x

PART 1
The Parenting Bit

Just When You Thought It Was About to Get Easier

Fact: it doesn't.

It's wincingly condescending to look back on any stage of life from your lofty position A Bit Further Along The Timeline, and tell the inexperienced and exhausted newbies, waaaay back near the start, how easy they have it.

'Ohhhh, I remember those days – you enjoy it! It all gets SO much harder when you're at MY stage.'

Oh, do kindly fuck off.

There should be a law that anyone giving it the 'just you wait' spiel to a sunken-eyed mother battling a toddler and a baby around Sainsbury's in a double buggy, without clearing the entire bottom shelf of the 'mugs and glasses' aisle with the edge of the buggy-board or throwing her offspring into the recycling bins at the door, should get a pogo stick rammed up their arse.

EVERY stage of parenting is hard. Whatever stage you're

at it sucks. Pregnancy sucks. Toddlers suck. Tweenagers suck. Adolescents suck – or try to. The whole thing is basically one long SUCKY SUCK from cradle to 'what do you *mean* you want to come back and live at home when you've finished university? GO AWAY.'

The Middle Years bring some especially sucky horrors with them that I didn't foresee until they crept into my life, knackering me in new sucky ways.

What follows is a possibly exhausting but certainly not exhaustive list of some of the main offenders I struggled with, that took me by surprise and caused me at one time or another to look back and allow myself a sneaky, private moment of…

'Shit, I wish I'd known just how lovely and easy it was when they were young!!'

Then I hit myself in the face with one of my son's canoe-sized football boots, remember how lucky I am, and get on with it.

Missing

When our children are very young, it's easy, and perfectly understandable, to feel as if we're living in the deepest pit of Hell.

We think that nothing could EVER come even close to the hellishness of this Hell, except if our father-in-law came round for tea and pointed out how we should just relaaaax more.

The temptation to abandon our children in a petrol station forecourt with a packet of Skips to keep them going and a note saying 'Out of Order' taped to their dungarees can be overwhelming, when we haven't slept for five years and just want TO SIT DOWN IN SILENCE FOR A WHOPPING THIRTY SECONDS AND REMEMBER WHAT BEING A HUMAN FEELS LIKE.

These brutal Early Years, suffocating us slowly from all sides like a gigantic, infected pustule of tantrums, laundry and human excrement, have the unfortunate side-effect of somewhat overshadowing the beauty and wonder and loveliness of life with young children.

So many times I wished those years were over. Over and over.

And over again.

We all do.

'Christ, I can't WAIT until they grow up!' I'd wail, picking glitter out of the crevices in my forehead, folding mountains of tiny items of clothing, reading *The Gruffalo* with all the voices for the thousandth time until my neck snapped and my eyes turned to dust and crumbled onto the *Star Wars* duvet cover, taking the nappy bins out, scraping the scrambled egg off the kitchen floor and trying to get a rain cover to stay ON THE DAMNED BUGGY.

I cannot WAIT until this is over, I thought.

But what we don't appreciate, because humans never do until it's too late and it's gone, is what we have.

This is a huge shame.

Because one day, it IS over.

Something is gone.

Missing.

The Middle Years is one of the first times we feel The Missing, and it can hit HARD. Like every other parent I know who's been through this stage of family life, I realised one day – probably just after I watched a toddler giggling to the point of wetting herself as her dad blew giant raspberries on her cheeks – that I was missing something; and quite simply, it was the irreplaceable joy of the Early Years.

God, I missed it!

I missed the smiles and giggles, the chuckles and toothless grins.

I missed getting a handful of chubby ankles and kiss-me cheeks.

I missed being able to actually *kiss* those kiss-me cheeks without the kiss being wiped off IMMEDIATELY, lest anyone contract Mummy Leprosy.

I missed hearing, 'Mummy, look what I've made!'

I missed being able to please them.

If I'm honest, I think I missed being needed, wanted, and feeling hugely loved and appreciated.

By the age of twelve or so, my kids could look at me with eyeballs emitting all the hatred, shame, pity, rage and disgust it's possible for one person to muster, and shoot it all at me like a burning dagger to the long-wilted maternal heart.

Before breakfast.

And yes. It hurt.

But it's normal. They're kids growing up and testing everything – especially us.

Even if we know all this, it doesn't make it much easier to bear when it's in your knackered face every day, and you've just especially gone to the effort of making them the exact dinner they said they love more than any other dinner in the world, and then went and made a tit of yourself by trying valiantly to help with their Year 3 maths homework and forgetting that 25 x 3 is actually not 62.

It's hard, because you miss them for who, and how, they once were.

I wish I'd known then that The Missing is a very normal part of being a parent with slightly older children, was happening to everyone else I knew too, and to just get on and enjoy the stage we were at, for what it was.

My kids didn't love me any less, and at least they were still *there*, the gobby little shits.

And, one day, they wouldn't be.

Full Empty Nest Syndrome

This is a perfect example of 'the worst of both worlds' – and, because you're super-smart, you'll have figured out already that this isn't an ideal set-up.

Good ol' empty nest syndrome is what most parents experience when their kids leave home.

Full empty nest syndrome is when the kids have left YOU, emotionally and in all loving, sweet ways, but are selfish and needy enough (and twelve-years-old enough) to still live at home and force you to pay for the lever-arch files and drive them to gymnastics club every Monday. But NOT TALK TO THEM WHEN THEY ARE WITH THEIR FRIENDS.

It's an especially cruel situation, because far from being able to move on, give the nest a good clear-out and maybe move a treadmill into their old bedroom so you can look at it every day and think about maybe using it, and allow yourself some time to get over the feeling of loss for something you miss, it's there in your face.

Every day. Eating cornflakes. Playing *Fortnite*.

The nest isn't empty.

It's still full; full of reminders of how things were, and how different they are now.

And we have to live IN it, constantly.

Constantly reminded of the joy... just out of reach.

When the joy goes, and it does because life has the habit of moving on and you can't do finger-painting with a twelve-year-old who wants to play *Minecraft* with his mates, it feels like a bereavement.

Really, it does.

Obviously we don't really wish the knackering, snot-infested stink-fest of the Early Years back. But it doesn't mean we don't miss *aspects* of it.

It took me years to realise that the new 'heaviness' I started to feel when my children were a little older – a kind of deep, unfathomable sadness that I thought might be depression, or midlife crisis or the wrong kind of under-eye cream (and was probably a combination of all of those) – was also a deep, unspoken, unrecognised, unnamed grief at the loss of something magical and beautiful, purely and totally, unashamedly, freely HAPPY.

And I'd never really get that back.

Those young children were gone now.

Their faces had changed, bodies had morphed into someone else's, voices had dropped, teeth had been straightened, moods had altered and characters had transformed.

They were new people.

Part of the Middle Years of parenting is slowly getting to know these new people.

Meeting them. Talking with them.

Finding out what they like.

What they believe in.

What they dream of.

Who they are, separate to us.

Even the people they are right now will keep changing throughout their lives.

I sometimes think the Middle Years are thrown in as a long, slow goodbye to the people we gave birth to and nurtured, taught and made plasticine animals with, helped and loved.

I've fallen in love with the 'new them', obviously, and I adore them. They're amazing people, changing all the time, and impressing and inspiring me with all the things they can do now. Often much better than me.

But it doesn't mean I don't miss who they were when they were little, and who WE were, both individually and as a family, back then.

Those days will never come back.

Skip forward a few years to when the nest really *is* empty – something that happens shockingly fast – and you'll wish you could be lucky enough to only be suffering from Full Empty Nest Syndrome again.

Just to hear a bedroom door slam once, choke in a cloud of overpowering deodorant wafting through the bathroom door, trip on a wet towel lying across the landing floor, put away eight packets of open cereal every morning and curse all the hair that's blocking the plug hole.

Because at least then they were still there.

I wrote a little song about all this ages ago, and it still makes me cry. It made a lot of people I sang it to cry as well, but that might have been because I was playing the ukulele while I sang it, and I can't play the ukulele.

Anyway, it goes like this:

A Love Song for My Children – *Please Stop Doing That*

From the moment that I met you, you've been fucking up my life.
You ripped my perineum like a 9 lb human knife.
You bit my nipples till they bled and threw up in my lap,
And refused to stand or sit or walk until you broke my back,
And I'd say…
Darling, please stop doing that.

You woke me every morning, by sitting on my head.
With a nappy filled with urine, you'd sprawl across my bed.
You'd knee me in the stomach, and with an innocent little look,
You'd smack me in the eyeball with the corner of a hardback book,
And I'd say…
Darling, it's 5 a.m.… please stop doing that.

You spat out all the dinner that I lovingly prepared,
You said you'd 'only eat my toast if you cut it into squares!'
I did exactly as you asked, and shaved off all the crusts,
And you took one look at them and screamed: 'BUT I WANTED TRIANGLES!'
(NOTHING rhymes with 'triangles'. Sorry.)
And I'd say…
Darling, please stop doing that.

You ate me out of house and home and then demanded more.
The towels from our bathroom lived, soaking, on your floor.
You used my best mascara, and lost my favourite shoes,
And then you had the gall to come and say, 'Mum, can I have some money please for Zac's party because everyone is bringing drink and I don't want to be bullied about it, and can you pick me up at about midnight – NOT BEFORE – because he lives in a village somewhere and I think it's like ten miles away or something and there are no buses, but I can't talk about it right now because Holly's FaceTiming me about what she's wearing tonight…'
And I'd say…
Darling, please stop doing that.

[NOTE: at this point the music goes into a minor key to denote GREAT SADNESS AND TRAGEDY, after a period of time has passed and life has moved on. Please read accordingly. Thank you.]

I wake up every morning, so near you, but alone.
This house has lost the heartbeat that made a house a home.
I can't go in your bedroom, and you think you're getting fat,
And the only way I can talk to you is via WhatsApp chat.

I invite you for the weekend, but my offers are refused.
The car is in the driveway, redundant and unused.
There's a fridge full of your favourites, but there's no one here to eat them.
My arms are waiting for your hugs, but there's no one here to greet them.
And I say…
Darling, please come back.
Please come back and do all that.

Living in Limbo

Here's a fun little game of 'good news/bad news' that Life plays with us in the Middle Years:

Good news: our kids don't need or want us so much any more. Hurrah! Freedom! Pack your bags, baby, we're off. Paris or Rio?

Bad news: we can't go anywhere, because they still need and want us just enough to require us to stay put.

This is the glorious state of Limbo. And it lasts about… ten years.

Here's an interesting little historical factoid for you, should you enjoy such things:

Limbo was actually a place, not a back-breaking dance made popular by the unexpectedly bendy Chubby Checker in 1962, and best performed at a party after twelve tequila slammers and a bet.

The word derives from the Latin 'limbus', OBVIOUSLY, meaning 'edge', and was situated on the highly sought-after border regions of Hell.

And that's exactly where we find ourselves the moment our children head off to school to collect other people's bad habits and nits: the borders of Hell, but without the perks.

On the home front I found I was no longer wanted or needed on a minute-to-minute 'Help! I've shoved a pen lid up my nose!' level, because my children had rudely taken over my primary duties such as putting food into their mouths and making sure they didn't drink bleach or moon out of the front window when the postman comes.

I tried the 'Well in that case, since you seem to have things so well taken care of, I'm off' line, and got myself all ready to drive around the French Riviera in an open-topped car, pretending to know how to smoke Gitanes.

But no, despite the fact that my children ignored me 90 per cent of the time, I still wasn't free to go off and do my own thing because for some reason I was still responsible for their wellbeing, and Life continued to throw children's dental emergencies, mysterious twenty-four-hour vomiting bugs and the school run at me.

And thus it is:

Nobody wants us, but everyone wants us to stick around just in case they do, and especially to do their sweaty laundry and pick them up from parties at 3 a.m.

It's glorious.

We'll just have to cruise round the Riviera when we're eighty.

See you there.

The Authority Drain

I have no clout whatsoever in my family any more.

The hamster has more authority than me, and he's dead.

Honestly, nobody listens to a thing I say, unless it's, 'Cash! Food! Phone credit! Over here!'

To my children, I've become background white noise; a kind of low-level, whining 'YadayadayadayadaDishwasherYadaHomeworkYadayadaPICKUPYOURMESSblahblahblahPLEASEGOTOBEDNOW', while I get on with the small task of keeping the entire family alive, fed, in clean-ish underwear, and with a solid supply of A4 paper, USB cables and deodorant.

This 'losing all power and authority' happens to most of us when our children grow above three feet tall, and start developing annoying things like Their Own Ideas and Opinions.

It's an adjustment I don't mind admitting that I found not very easy at all.

When they were babies, I was right. Always. This is mainly because it's fairly easy to be right when the person you're arguing against can't tell night from day and spends most of their time trying to locate their own mouth, so they can shove their fingers into it.

I loved this stage. I was like Chairman Mao on nappy duty.

Even the pre-school years were a bit of a power trip because four-year-olds are still generally wrong about most things – or at least I could *tell* them they were, and unsubtly suggest/force them to do things differently (where 'differently' meant 'my way').

If Mummy's Rules were broken then I, The All-Powerful One With Sole Access To The Doughnuts Kitty, could enforce cruel punishments such as switching off the Wi-Fi and withholding squeezy yoghurt pouches for an afternoon.

I WIN.

But slowly, it changes.

They change.

They start to be right. (Or think they are. And can rationally articulate as much.)

And we, the ones who have grown, nurtured, comforted, cleaned, worried about, baked tiger birthday cakes for and loved for years, are now little more than objects of intense irritation, stupidity, inconvenience, embarrassment and dismay, getting between them and Popularity Nirvana.

And this is just the start.

Teflon Teens

Teenagers grow lots of things on their bodies that neither they nor we want to talk about very much.

One of these is an impenetrable, bullet-proof, non-stick layer of Not Giving A Shit that covers their entire being, tends to develop around their twelfth birthday, and is used as a shield against all parental input.

It's extraordinarily effective.

Government Defence departments should really get on board with it.

Things that don't work:

- **Reasoning** – it's hard to reason with someone whose hair is pasted over their eyes to hide their disdain.
- **Punishment** – teenagers have recently clubbed together on social zit-sharing sites and invented these crazy, new-fangled things called Opinions

and Human Rights, and use these to strike the fear of death into us by following Childline on Twitter.

- **Shouting at them** – they don't care, you look and feel pathetic, then you get angry with *yourself*, and finally you feel guilty. FAB. They're also probably Insta-storying it live, the bastards.
- **Crying** – it might look as if they care for a brief moment, but most often that's because they want money, or clothes, or money, or a phone top-up, or money.
- **Withholding pocket money** – absolutely no point. They'll just sell naked photos of themselves to the Sixth Formers for a tenner each.
- **Sending them to their room** – they think this is the best thing ever, as it means a) being away from you and b) being closer to their mates on Snapface.

***

Due to this phenomenally irritating ability to not give a shit about anything we do, say, want, like or feel, teenagers are invincible.

You can't break something that can't be broken; it's like trying to smash air, and you look really stupid trying.

The only thing we can do is to meet Teflon with Teflon: don't give a shit about *their* not giving a shit.

This has the triple advantage of taking away all the power they think they might have over you, annoying them and making you feel smug.

Just ignore, relent and wait for it all to pass.

About twenty years usually does it.

They still love you.

They just won't realise it until their own children reject them too, and your persistent cough suggests they might be getting closer to getting their hands on some of their inheritance.

I Am a Teenager's Worst Parent

One of the great ironies of parenting is that the worst people to parent teenagers, are the parents of teenagers.

Someone really should have thought that one through a lot better when designing the whole Life Arc thing. It's unhelpfully shoddy work.

The reason for this incompatibility, though, is simple: teenagers, despite their attempts at bullish defiance and independence, still need almost constant, consistent and unconditional support, love and delicate handling. They need to be looked after by people who are strong, secure in themselves, patient, understanding, calm, happy and rational.

But, by an amazing stroke of unfortunate coincidence and basic maths, by the time our children are teenagers we have been a parent for at least thirteen years, and biology has cunningly arranged it such that the moment anyone has been a parent for thirteen years, they turn into a screaming, insecure, angry, self-destructive, irrational witch, with the added benefits of mania, hormonal breakdown, insanity, misery, impatience, uncontrollable anger, hatred, financial problems and saggy arm skin.

This set-up makes it nearly impossible to do something as simple as crossing a road, without being hit by one of Life's articulated lorries, let alone negotiate the terrifying minefield of broken teenage hearts, online bullying, GCSE options, acne and not having the latest phone.

We can't possibly be of any use to our children at this stage of their lives, because, by this stage, our own are in such a goddam mess we can barely get dressed without having a major existential crisis.

As a result, we make a spectacular pig's ear of the whole thing – just as most parents have done as long as parents have existed.

If they had ANY shred of decency or kindness, our teenaged children would take themselves off to live in a youth hostel for a few years, to give us the space we need.

It's not you, it's... you. And them. And all of it.

Try to be kind to yourself.

One day they'll have their own children and realise that you were just doing your best, at this time, in this stage, in this YOU that you are now.

And that'll have to do.

Big School; Big Changes

Going up to secondary school is a HUGE deal.

I didn't realise how huge, until it happened to my eldest.

The change, not just for her, but for the whole family, was enormous. And enormously unexpected.

I received a few emails asking me to buy 175 A4 ring binders and a calculator that cost more than a week in Devon at half term, and was sent some code or other for the school lockers and a new password for the maddeningly complicated online lunch payment system, but the gigantic emotional and practical upheaval of moving from primary to secondary was barely mentioned even once.

Compare this with the DELUGE of information, preparation, focus and intense worry-mongering that went on when they started in Reception class or went up into Year 1, to the point where most of us were cacking our drawers about it all.

Meetings with teachers, slow, careful integration into the classroom, smelling their coat peg and deciding whether to put a cat or a unicorn on their book tray – the whole thing was managed in a layer of cotton wool so thick it was hard to see the school gates.

But for secondary, it's basically a case of: Right. Off you fuck, then.

And that goes for both the pupils and their baffled parents.

The school gate slams shut in your face, and our kids disappear into a world into which it feels as if we suddenly have no window, no access and no invitation.

And it's REALLY weird.

The main changes I wish I'd known about, are these:

- You'll probably NEVER do the school run again.
- Don't even THINK of going within ¼ mile of the playing field in case you're spotted, and your child dies of shame.
- From now on you'll only see other parents at teacher–parent evenings, when you'll all pretend that your kid is either far smarter or far more stupid than they really are, depending on how smart or stupid they actually are, or at fundraising wine-tasting events where you all get so smashed you don't know who anyone is anyway.
- It can have a pretty major effect on your child's mental wellbeing. One of my children, who had always been confident, happy and outgoing, developed what were basically panic attacks for the

first term of secondary school. I'd get a call almost every day by 9.30 a.m. to say X child was already in the nurse bay and was feeling sick. Or had been sick. Or was about to be sick. Basically, there was suddenly a LOT of talk about sick. I knew for a fact that there was absolutely nothing physically wrong with this child at ALL. It was purely a case of anxiety and panic. It took most of the first term, but it all eventually settled down. It's pretty common, and it's worth being prepared for in case you start getting The Phone Calls of Sick the second you sit down to work.

- Everything changes in secondary school. Including your child. It's like they get an upgrade or something, when they start term. New friends you've never heard of; a whole new language they suddenly speak; new hobbies and interests they were never into before. New moods. New hairstyles. New attitude. It's a bit of a shocker, and for a while it feels as if they've been replaced by someone else. But they're still there. Just under the new, chemically enhanced hair.
- Homework gets a bit… heavy. Not straight away, but it's like *actual* homework, as opposed to drawing farts coming out of farm animals or learning to add 4 bananas to 5 bananas and getting something

near-ish a 9-banana split. It also requires our help sometimes, which not only annihilates most of our free evening time, but is also almost guaranteed to make us look really stupid. (See 'I know nothing'.)

Losing Control

While we're at it, here are a few more things I lost control of when my kids grew higher than my nipples (or 'waist-height', as it's now known), went off to Big School and started to become their own little selves:

What they eat. There I'd been since the day they were born, trying to feed them well, eat family meals together like Good Families do, and put carrots in front of them so they could learn to accurately throw them at the fridge. And here I was now, smugly admiring my scurvy-free kids, who knew that eating crap is bad for you.

Which was exactly when they started wanting to eat nothing but crap.

Even if they didn't eat the crap in front of me, they'd sneak it under the radar in their school bag/coat/bra/giant trainers, and when I finally got around to hoovering their teen-pit I'd uncover the European Wrapper Mountain under the bed.

Eighteen Haribo packets. That was our record.

I did genuinely find it a bit heart-breaking to see my kids filling their bodies with junk, but you know what? They're gonna do it, however much organic Jamie Oliver we've rammed down their toddler throats.

And if they do, they do. All their mates are probably growing up on Tangfastics too.

THAT SAID, if they feel bad about what they're eating, or get down about how it's making them feel or look or just *be* in themselves, that's a whole different matter, and worth keeping an eye out for. They can hopefully come and talk to you about it, and you can help them 'clean up' a bit, in a way that works for them.

Just best not to scream and shout at them about it. It'll almost certainly make things worse.

***

What they're interested in. Right, so obviously it's fantastic that our kids have different interests and hobbies and talents and obsessions to ours. It's one of the things I love most about being a mum – seeing how different my children all are from me, and from each other.

BUT FUCK ME, I HAVE LIMITS, HONEY.

Computer programming or anything to do with coding?

No. Just no. I can't even pretend.

I can't even fake a modicum of anything that resembles ANY interest or understanding or zzzzzzzzzzzz, nope, sorry, you've lost me.

If it were films or travel or photography or dance or skateboarding or cooking or books or tattoo design or the weird sticky feet of Peruvian tree frogs, or ANYTHING I can share an interest in, I'M IN.

I'll take you to all the clubs and buy the kit and order all the books and get TOTALLY INTO IT with you.

But, Sweetheart, if you want to spend your afternoons programming the computer you just made from scratch using old bits of metal reclaimed from a supermarket skip to create a rotating 3-D model of a soup spoon, I'm going to go walk outside and leave you to it.

For two years.

***

What they watch. I've sat through more episodes of one wincingly shit sitcom or other that still reduces my kids to tears of hilarity on the 700th viewing, than I care to count. Just sit through it, laugh occasionally, and go on Twitter when they're not looking.

***

What they read. All those books you leave lying around everywhere because they're GOOD and you SO must read this because it's incredible and it will change your life and it's a classic (and, subtle subtext, I LOVE IT so I want you to love it too)?

They won't want to read any of them.

They'll read whatever *they* want. Probably about aliens or snot or aliens with guns that shoot snot.

But y'know what: IF THEY'RE READING AT ALL, or even know what a book IS, then that's GREAT.

***

The friends they keep. Bit of a clash-zone, this one, but that's normal. Some kids deliberately choose friends they don't even like, just because they know we'll hate them.

Telling them their friends are assholes doesn't usually help. It just makes them hate YOU, not the asshole kid.

Subtly avoiding all playdates and invitations to birthday parties can work, but it takes dedication and serious stealth-blocking. In the end, though, they choose their own mates. Even if they ARE assholes. And hopefully one day they'll just decide to hang out with nicer kids.

Speaking of assholes…

Honesty

One of the lovely things we can do with our kids as they get older is finally be HONEST with them about loads of things we sort of... had to put a fairy-tale, politically correct gloss on when they were little.

One of those is what we *actually* think about other people. Including their mates.

When they're very young we teach our kids to be nice to others. It's sort of the baseline/generally accepted way to behave in a civil society, and I guess that makes it a reasonably good starting point.

We gently lie at nursery about how sweet Hugo is, even though we know he's a selfish little twat who doesn't share, pulls hair and just caused grievous bodily harm to your kid's brand new Peppa Pig.

'Oh, it was just an accident, honey,' we say consolingly, slapping on the bullshit whitewash. 'I'm sure he didn't MEAN to.'

Oh yes he fucking did.

Enter the Middle Years truth-bomb about HUGO, and all Hugos:

Hugo is a cunt.

And the truth is that quite a lot of people are cunts too, honey.

People-pleasing, trying to be friends with everycunt and always trying to see their nice side can go take a running jump when our kids are older.

They deserve the truth.

Here's a little poem I wrote for my children, to make this clearer. I think I'm going to make T-shirts with the title printed right across the front in size seventy-two font, and hand them out at the next school Sport's Day.

Some People Are Just Cunts

Be nice to people, my mummy said,
and always give a smile.
Help them, when they need it.
Go the extra mile.
Lend a hand when times are hard,
A laugh when it seems needed.
Listen, care, and give yourself
Without it being pleaded.
Well.
I've done all this for forty years.
I've been a lovely friend.
I've trusted, helped and listened well,
Right up to the end.
I've held their hands and offered hugs, and often borne the brunts.
And I've learned a thing to teach you kids:
Some people are just cunts.

But I Was Your Age Just the Other Day

One of the weirdest things about being the parent of kids who are older than about eight, is it's the first stage of their lives that we remember being, ourselves.

Not just what we think we 'remember' from blurred, overexposed photos in dusty albums, or from told and retold family stories of how we were taken to the beach for the first time and three hours later we shat a whole nappy full of dry sand, and oh how everyone laughed! We don't *remember* that. We remember the story.

But we *can* actually remember being the age our children are now.

What we felt, thought and did.

This trip down Memory Lane is not only deeply uncomfortable for those of us who were unspeakably cringeworthy geeks and whose emergency tampon supply fell out of her bag in geography and was used by half the class as ammunition to throw at Mr Jenkins, it also brings us face-to-sagging-face with the fact that, if our children are that old, we are now a long way down the road to losing our bladder control, teeth and marbles.

It doesn't matter how many years pass: in my head, I still think/hope/pretend I'm somewhere between seventeen and seventeen and a half, and I don't imagine this will change until I'm well into my sixties, a decade in which I plan to become a fabulously stylish, fascinating sex bomb. *Naturellement.*

I'M NOT IN MY FORTIES! Not this girl. When my mother was forty I thought she was ancient.

Forty?!

Forty was FOR MUMS.

(Oh. I see.)

So now here I am. In MY forties and living in a house with offspring who are the same age as I still vividly remember being. Got to admit, reader, this brought on a SLIGHT sensation of epic identity confusion and existential panic.

I felt both reassuringly young and depressingly old.

Both a teenager and mother.

It's an odd shift, when your 'babies' are suddenly taller than you, look like you, do their own laundry, deal with periods and boy/girlfriends and homework deadlines and hangovers… it really does bring the two of you very slightly into the same 'Life Bracket' for the first time.

They're in that fuzzy hand-over zone of childhood-meets-adulthood, and it's the first time there's a bit of overlap between your remembered experiences and their life now. I guess it's just part of the gradual and constant shift in your relationship over time.

It might not feel it when they wince every time you breathe and scream 'I HATE YOU!!' from the bathroom, but, as our children get older, we're actually getting closer to them.

Maybe not in age or character, but closer in life, and things we can talk about, share, argue over, agree on, and help each other through.

And that's one of the nicest things about the Middle Years.

Family Holidays

In the Middle Years it's the rule that all family holidays must be deeply unpleasant, exhausting, financially ruinous, damp, mentally crushing endurance tests, requiring a holiday – ALONE – immediately upon our return.

In any other context, such suffering would elicit an emergency call to Amnesty International.

For the best part of a decade, every single one of our family holidays contained at least one child who was grumpy, ill, missing their mates too much to be able to have any fun, studying for one bloody load of exams or another, having a sulk-off with one sibling or other, cursing the slowness of the Wi-Fi, pissed off that they'd left their Essential Holiday T-shirt at home, or going through something puberty-related that I didn't want to think about.

In the middle of our Middle Years, somewhere between a year I can't remember and another one I've chosen to forget, we decided to be extremely fashionable and skint, and have a Staycation.

Thus we dutifully spent five hours stuck in stationary traffic on the M5 motorway, eating service station Ginsters pasties and pointing at the ugly people in the stationary cars next to ours, also eating Ginsters pasties.

The holiday spirit was unmistakable.

After the happy journey we enjoyed a lovely week in Cornwall being reminded of the true beauty of rain in all its myriad forms, and also of the hideousness of other people's children. And dogs. And children with dogs.

And dog shit, mostly on our flip-flops.

My son went crabbing and was promptly bitten by a crab that didn't seem to like being thrown into a plastic bucket with thirty-five other angry crabs 400 times an hour, so he went to the car and cried.

My eldest sat alone on the beach reading a copy of *Shout* magazine, while attempting to tan the underside of her chin by reflecting the only two available rays of sunshine onto it using the back of a spoon she'd nicked from the motorway service station café. Shortly after this she announced that her Achilles tendon was fat and she wanted to kill herself.

My middle child, supportively, said at least her tendon wasn't as massive as her bum.

Eldest hit Middle Child with *Shout* magazine.

Middle Child threw *Shout* magazine into a rock pool.

Eldest threw Middle Child into the rock pool.

Middle Child got bitten by a crab and went to the car to cry with her brother.

I had no sex whatsoever for the entire week, which was a shame because it made it impossible to differentiate that holiday week from every other week of the previous five years.

To make everything better and more Summer Holiday-ish we built a campfire that evening.

We all vowed to go back again the next year and try to light it as well if the weather proved to be less shit, and use the glow of the flames to see the midges better.

It was all exactly as it should be.

And I really miss it.

Who the FUCK Said the F-word?

Most of us try to protect our kids from things that can hurt them.

Physical harm, mental harm, emotional harm, professional harm, financial harm, harmy harm.

We try to build their self-esteem and give them the confidence to be whoever they are, however they. Unless they're a twat, but, even then it's OK if they are *kind* twats.

And THEN. Some superfuckinghelpful wonderperson out there goes and opens their self-esteem-busting mouth and announces in the swimming pool changing room that, 'I'm so FAT!! Ugh!' and your whole, carefully implemented self-esteem parenting strategy is fucked.

I would like to kill the person who introduced my children to the concept that thighs could be fat, and that this was disgusting. (Especially when theirs were definitely not fat at all.)

Everything had been going great until then.

They had good appetites, ate pretty much everything

(except aubergine – totally with you there, kid) and some hummus their dad once made, that looked and smelled like cat vomit.

It was all very simple and reassuring.

Hungry: eat something.

Not hungry: don't eat something.

No food/fat/body-image-related conversations.

No discussions about the calorie content of everything from watermelon (low – we trust watermelon) to granola (surprisingly high – we are very suspicious of granola).

And then one day it happened; one of my children, then aged seven, announced that her tummy was fat.

She said this while kneading her beautiful little seven-year-old stomach skin like excess dough in a bowl.

ARRRRRGH!

I'd never used the word 'fat' in a derogatory way. Ever.

Marker pens were fat, cheques were fat (usually the ones I was signing for one flippin' expensive music lesson or other), lies were big *and* fat.

But people were never described as fat.

Even if their main, unmissable, most clearly identifiable physical attribute was their eye-popping, astounding fatness, I'd still not tell my kids they were fat.

But someone had planted the idea into *their* child's head, and, from there, via playground chitter-chatter and changing-room pointing, into *my* child's head, that tummies could be fat, and that a fat tummy was disgusting.

That someone was Ella's mum. I hated Ella's mum.

I knew I could never control Z, delete, undo, erase Ella's mum's fat-bomb. My daughter now knew about fat tummies, and that they were 'yucky'.

Outside influencing continues throughout our kids' lives, but the Middle Years are where most of it starts.

There's nothing we can do about it except lock our kids in a soundproof box or move to the Gobi Desert, or both.

Failing those convenient options, all we can do is explain that some people – like ELLA'S MUM – are clearly morons, and we love our kids JUST THE WAY THEY ARE, and just like Mark Darcy loved Bridget.

And that's the best love there is.

Honey, I Don't Like You Right Now

Sometimes I don't like one, or other or even any, of my children.

I felt wretched about this for about twelve minutes one Tuesday afternoon, and then realised I was wasting perfectly good eyebrow harvesting time, it's completely normal, and I should chill out about it.

They are, after all, just people. And people can sometimes be irritating or unkind or stubborn or selfish or dishonest or lazy or disinclined to hang their wet towels on the towel rail you specifically went to B&Q to buy and which is obviously there for this exact goddam purpose in order to prevent the towels from smelling rancid and rotting, and spreading thrush and athlete's foot and Weltschmerz all over the house.

It's different when they're little and aren't able to do much for themselves, bar shovelling food into their mouths and drawing amazingly accurate crayon drawings of lines of crayon, and bumble about in a cute way being adorable and chubby.

But as they get older and 'should know better', it gets easier to feel a true sense of dislike towards one's own child when they are being, well, frankly, hugely dislikeable.

Just because they're our children, doesn't make them exempt from this dislike.

I remember the first time I looked at one of my kids and thought, 'Yeah, you're a bit of a knob right now, to be honest, and I don't wanna hang around you.'

I felt pretty horrible about that for a while.

But as they all grew up and went through their various periods of being fairly unpleasant in one way or another, I realised it's perfectly normal to love and care for your child, and occasionally think they're a bit of a knob.

It usually passes when whichever school issue or emotional growth spurt or disastrous hair situation has resolved itself, so it's maybe best to keep your feelings to yourself, not worry about them, and wait until your child un-knobs again.

Oh, also…

You're My Favourite

At any one time, I have a favourite child.

There. I said it.

This changes according to who is being the most annoying/moody/pissy/hormonal/argumentative/frickin' irrational/bitchy/unresponsive to all forms of kind communication/generally just shit, at the time.

As I write this, I am forty-five years old and I have four children, aged twenty-two, nineteen, sixteen... and two. (Yeah. Bit of a gap there. Don't ask. It's all for another book.)

The toddler is just... doing what toddlers do. Mainly being a mixture of insanely cute and infuriatingly stubborn. But where the older three are concerned, it's fair to say that there's almost always one of them I'm getting on best with at any particular time, and would most like to hang out with.

I don't feel even remotely guilty about this. Any normal person likes one person more than another, even if all of them were grown inside the same body.

Just, y'know, try not to go around pinning a 'MUM'S FAVE CHILD' badge onto their hoodie.

And anyway, you know what? Sometimes my children don't like me.

That's cool. They have no obligation to.

They don't OWE me anything. I chose to make them, without even asking them.

Also, I'm a massive pain in the backside much of the time, and I wouldn't like me much either.

Sure, if they're NASTY, rude, ungrateful for something for which they should be grateful, thoughtless, unkind, etc., then of course I pull them up on it. Nobody likes people like that, and it's my job to try and steer them away from becoming one.

But if they don't like ME? That's fine. They are free to be who they are, and like who they like. And, at times, that might not include their parents.

Who's Nicked My Eyeliner?

You know you have teenagers in your house, when:

All your phone chargers have disappeared.

If you *do* manage to locate one, it doesn't fit your phone because you're the only member of the family who didn't get a new model within the last twenty minutes.

Ditto eyeliner, hair bands, black ankle socks and dry shampoo.

There are bags and rucksacks and satchels and totes everywhere.

There's a permanent trail of crumbs from the cereal cupboard to the kitchen door.

You can't get into the bathroom before 8.30 a.m., or between 8 and 10.30 p.m. Or all weekend.

The ratio of fresh air to deodorant in said bathroom will never exceed 1:25,000.

At certain times of the month it's best to move out for a few days, to avoid Oestrogen Death.

If you need to find your son's bed in order to wash his disturbingly crusty bedding, it's most likely to be under four feet of jeans, hoodies and electrical wires that don't appear to belong to anything in particular, but are all ESSENTIAL, MUM!

You can't open the front door thanks to the fifteen pairs of enormous shoes piled up approximately six inches from the shoe rack.

You'll occasionally scream when a huge person walks into the room and you thought it was just you and your kids at home – and then you realise the giant is actually your own child, and he's just two feet taller and a foot broader than he was last week.

Even though you went shopping yesterday there is no food in the house, except for half-empty packets of Oreos and something that promises to make your skin smoother.

There are five razors lying along the side of the bath, each in their own pool of rust, and none of them are either blunt, sharp, or claimed by anyone.

There's face-pack residue all over the bathroom taps. And floor. And towel rails.

There are no towels on the towel rails.

There are towels on all floors, helping to conceal some of the forest of tumbleweed balls of brushed-out hair.

You could build a hang-glider from all the sanitary-towel wrappers gathering dust behind the toilet door.

On your way to the kitchen you will trip over three guitar

cases, a skateboard, two basketballs, hair straighteners, eight computer cables, an amp, a school blazer and a pair of inexplicably expensive headphones.

Your purse develops an invisible cash-portal, through which the fivers you KNOW you just put there vanish inexplicably. Unfortunately this portal doesn't operate in reverse.

When you call your children down for dinner you get a Snapchat of their bum in return.

Hard cash is the only currency that works. For everything. Including cuddles.

Answering Back

Yet another inconvenient trait developed by children as they pass the six-year milestone, is an ability to use exasperating things like logic, facts and quotes they stole from some know-it-all in the playground, and use them to prove us wrong.

High on a dizzying headrush of new-found Right-ness, they decide that this is the time to start listening to what we're saying for the first time in their lives, noticing when we're spouting all the crap we've relied on to get them to sit in the buggy, go to sleep, finish their peas and not watch eight hours of *Brooklyn Nine-Nine*, and then start to come up with smart-arse, reasonable and well-argued comments to challenge us on it.

And I tell you, I don't like it.

It means I actually have to concentrate on what I'm saying, and there's a very good chance that I will have to back down on whatever it was I was trying to get them to do, or not do, for absolutely no reason whatsoever except that It Would Make My Life Easier.

This is SO infuriating there are no words for it.

So, I'll stop here.

Sibling Civil War

Rivalry; n:

'Competition for the same objective, or for superiority in the same field.'

Sibling Rivalry; n:

'OH FOR FUCK'S SAKE, WILL YOU TWO STOP WINDING EACH OTHER UP?? JUST GIVE HER THE FRICKIN' TENNIS BALL, OK?!'

***

Throughout their lives, most siblings helpfully try to fill their parents' otherwise deathly boring lives with the joys of migraines and despair, by competing constantly with each other, pointlessly winding each other up, and arguing over things which couldn't possibly be less important.

In the Early Years, sibling rivalry is pretty simple and generally about one of only two things:

Attention – specifically, yours. And most specifically yours when you can't possibly give it, creating the perfect opportunity to demonstrate this parenting failure by pouring Diet Coke into the fish tank.

Possession – of everything from toys to bagels to the space on MY SIDE OF THE CAR, MUM!

There are spats and tiffs, some hair-pulling, maybe a scrap after a new Lego Star Wars figurine is found arranged in a sexually compromising position with a lucky Sylvanian. Maybe some dramatic sulking over who got the bigger ice cream. And that was that.

It all starts from day one of Siblinghood – programmed in, and good to go.

The second your back is turned towards a new Baby Sibling, Older Sibling starts destroying the entire house in a way he's never previously shown any interest in doing, and always at a time when you are completely incapable of doing anything about it because you have Baby Sibling's mouth around your nipple, or her stinking nappy half removed and dangerously close to your new trousers.

There you are, elbow deep in liquid shit… and Older Sibling will 'accidentally' stand three feet in front of you and 'accidentally' pour a pint of blackcurrant juice onto the rug in the hall. While 'accidentally' looking straight at you. And smiling.

And lo! Older Sibling has successfully won your attention back.

This is how it starts.

And *oh* how it gets worse.

The screeching and fighting that can occur over a plastic fireman's helmet or a scrap of tissue that neither of them wants IN THE SLIGHTEST, makes the Hundred Years War look like a lovers' tiff.

But fight over them, they will.

Objects demonstrate ownership, power and importance. Most of the castles in the world were built solely to exhibit all the useless but impressively huge objects won by kings with tiny penises.

'But LOOK! I have 700 helmet-cleaners!! Mwahahahaa, I RULE EVERYTHING.'

Objects are extra-desirable for children, because they can also be used as blunt instruments with which to dent Younger Sibling's skull.

And it doesn't stop there. A successful ruler soon learns that he or she needs to own not only things, but also SPACE.

Just when you thought you'd sorted out the whingeing over who has whose favourite blunt pencil, things move on to who is in whose AIR.

He's in MY room! She's on MY chair! He's breathing MY OXYGEN! Her fart just wafted into MY AURA!

And so on and on. Petty squabbles and tiresome whingeing.

It's exhausting. It's pointless. It's maddening. It pushes us ever closer to dropping an anvil onto their head from the first-floor window, if only we had an anvil. Or could be arsed.

BUT… move forward ten years, my friend, and these rivalries seem like child's play.

(Mainly because they are.)

When our children progress to the new battleground of secondary school, sibling rivalry turns into something far, far more complicated, more upsetting, and more difficult for us to sort out.

Enter, Sibling Civil War.

'War' is defined as a prolonged conflict. The key word here being 'prolonged'.

Gone are the happy days when a quick whack on the head with a building block is forgotten within minutes.

Older kids don't have quick-fix spats; they have serious long-term hostilities and painful, silent stand-offs.

They have Great Wars, and harboured resentments that can last for weeks.

Jealously, rage, hatred, resentment – they're in it for the big prize, baby.

Forget, 'She took my ruler!' Now it's, 'She looked at me in a shitty, condescending way, she's a bitch and I'm never going to watch her Insta stories again.'

Trying to sort out arguments over how someone looks at someone else, how they breathed, how loudly they did or didn't shut a door and whether it implied a deep-rooted, bitchy jealousy or not, is a little more complicated than asking someone to hand the ball back please.

It not only drives me mad much of the time, it tires me the fuck out.

The arguments themselves are wearing enough, and require intense, slow negotiations between the two warring factions, usually through closed doors and always involving you being wrong most of the time.

Worse, though, is when there's no argument at all – just an ATMOSPHERE of silent warring. Arguments and points made in a suffocating soup of silence.

Silent warring is heavy. It lumbers along, dragging the issue out and infecting the whole house until the air is weighed down with its hate-laden pauses and unspoken bloodbaths.

Two of my kids had a silence-off for months. It was like living in a glass-house full of eggshells, on ice.

At least once a week I felt like throwing myself onto the floor, arms flailing and screaming:

OH CHRIST, JUST SORT IT OUT. THIS IS FUCKING UNBEARABLE. CAN'T YOU JUST BE NICE TO EACH OTHER??

It's all completely normal when children start turning into young adults, with young adult problems, and awkward young adult relationships with other awkward young adults.

For the younger siblings, watching the older ones pull away and turn into independent, self-sufficient, often pensive or emotionally confusing grown-up people with 'complicated issues', can be hard.

There's a separation that was never there before – both physical, as they retreat into their bedrooms or to friends' houses ever more, and emotional, as the worries and thoughts they battle with are ever less comprehensible to their younger siblings: university options, sexuality, political awareness, need for solitude and space, and snogging.

For the first time in years, siblings in the Middle Years often don't inhabit the same 'stage of life' any more, and their circle of interests, abilities and concerns don't overlap very much.

The girl who used to play Guess Who with her brother and sister all afternoon and then let them plait her hair now wants to be alone in her room all weekend, and won't speak to anyone unless that someone is the person she has decided might get their hand in her pants at the next party.

She locks the bathroom door for hours and emerges in a shroud of body spray and self-consciousness, goes jogging and has weird food fads every few weeks.

Brothers start growing facial fluff, their voices drop, they want to be left alone to write song lyrics for people they fancy, and masturbate, and stand in front of the mirror admiring the ridiculous quiff they've constructed on their giant, spotty head.

Honestly, it broke a little piece of my maternal heart to see my kids, who used to laugh, play, giggle, bake muffins, adventure, read, sleep and grow together, become separated by emotional differences, incompatible wishes and desires, a difference in ages that just… got in the way of it all.

It's not the case all the time, of course.

Being older means they can do lots of new things together that they couldn't before: they can cycle into town, go shopping together, help each other with homework and friendship problems, give advice and support, and be almost adult-like in their communication and relationship.

Siblings in the teenage years can be the strongest source of support they have. Where parents are just annoying and DON'T UNDERSTAND, siblings do.

And there are still giggles at dinner, and days when everyone gets on like civilised humans, and fluffy moments of togetherness. They still have sleepovers in each other's rooms, film nights together on the sofa, advise on wardrobe dilemmas and hair crises and share GIFs of people falling into hedges. It's just yet another change that happens as people grow up, reshape, and the family dynamic changes yet again.

You get used to it. Just as they're about to leave home.

Parenting Truth-bombs

YOU'LL SAY ALL THE THINGS YOU HATED YOUR MUM SAYING TO YOU

You'll hear it coming out of your stupid parenting mouth, like a grim reflection in a sound mirror, and you'll hate yourself immediately, because you suddenly remember how much you hated hearing it when you were a kid, and now YOU are the source of that hate in your own kids, and... oh bollocks, how did this happen when you swore it wouldn't?!

Sometimes you can even feel it *before* it's fallen out of your mouth, bubbling on your tongue, and you know it's gonna come and you try to swallow it, catch it on the back of your front teeth... no... don't say it, don't... just... wait...

'HOW DARE YOU TALK TO ME LIKE THAT, I'm your MOTHER!'

DAMN. There it is, though. The words you swore YOU would never say – said.

And there will be more.

We're all going through the same midlife parenting stuff, just as they did, their mums did, and our kids will when they are parents too.

CHILDREN ARE HAPPY WHEN WE ARE HAPPY

I was told this recently by a psychotherapist, and it had never really occurred to me before.

About three seconds after I'd heard it I realised how OBVIOUS it was. (As with most obvious things whose obviousness we suddenly notice, in fact.)

It was one of the most guilt-alleviating, pressure-relieving, helpful concepts I'd ever heard, and I wish I'd learned it, and BELIEVED IT, years and years ago.

That's why I'm telling you now, so you know it.

I think I, like many of us, was so fixated on making my children happy, on the purpose and focus and centre of everything in my life being about THEM and their well-being, what THEY were doing in their lives, how happy THEY were, that I totally forgot to notice how much my own problems, anxieties, moods, rages, tears and general emotional fuck-handedness were affecting them. And not in a good way.

Whatever choices we might make, whatever decisions, circumstances out of our control, events or changes, whatever we may have done in our lives before or after having our children, if we are happy, and radiate that happiness towards our kids, it's more likely that they will be happy.

Growing Up Online

Right, here we go.

SCREEN TIME. The banest bane of every modern parent's LIFE.

Social media, online bullying, Instagram fakery, comparison, stress, bad posture, blindness, addiction, obesity, sexting, piles...

Danger danger danger danger... DANGER!!!!!!

So let's get this thorny little bastard dealt with.

Below are some thoughts, based solely on what I've observed, learned and cocked up over these years.

Basically, there seems to be mass confusion about the mass confusions and amassed, confused dangers, or otherwise, of SCREENY THINGS and all the terrifying things they either contain or can access.

I can't tell you how many TV and radio debates, online discussions, news stories and magazine shit-stirs I've taken part in, in which terrified, angry, outraged, catastrophising parents – usually wearing hazmat suits double-wrapped in kitchen foil in case any radiation from the smartphones in all our pockets might somehow explode their hippocampus during the interview – tell me how dangerous and damaging the online world is for our kids.

DO I KNOW WHAT THE INTERNET DOES TO OUR CHILDREN'S WELLBEING??!

Do I know the myriad dangers of smartphones?

Do I know they can talk to people who are not actually the people they think they are talking to, and some of those people might be Bad People?

Do I know that social media was specifically invented to harm children?

Do I know that the light from one tablet screen can keep a village of 400 children awake for seven months?

Do I know that obesity, diabetes, misery, low self-esteem and cellulite all come from Instagram?

Do I know that fresh air is good for children?

Do I know that my child's likelihood of self-harming is about... well... I'm not sure EXACTLY but it's definitely much higher if you have Netflix in your house.

DO I NOT CARE ABOUT THESE THINGS?!

Well, yes, I do care. I don't especially want my kids to be depressed, self-harming, self-loathing recluses who hook up with child molesters in chat rooms, if I'm really honest.

I quite want them to be happy and healthy.

I want them to go outside and play.

And eat fruit.

I want them to be nice to other people.

And nice to themselves.

I want them to read *A Room with a View* and cry because it's so beautiful and they know their life will never be the same again until they are kissed in a cornfield.

I want them to be able to come and talk to me if they have any concerns, and know they won't be judged or told off.

But...

I also want them to be a part of the world in which they live, and this, after a certain age, does generally involve owning a smartphone.

I wish it didn't, just as it hadn't when they were toddlers (my older children are lucky enough to have been born in the very last gasp of Human existence before the smartphone invasion).

But this is the world my teenagers live in NOW. And I want them to be able to communicate with their friends in the way that Kids These Days Do, even if it's not how I did it.

I want them to use the Internet to help with their schoolwork, and answer the billion questions they might have about history or genetics or fashion or things they haven't even heard of until they go on the Internet and see them.

I *want* them to be allowed to use Snapchat.

And Instagram.

And to watch Netflix. SOMETIMES EVEN IN THEIR BEDROOM.

Most of the worries we have about any of this, is that it's NOT WHAT WE KNEW.

Most of us hardly recognise or feel any connection with loads of things that the New Teenage World contains or involves.

So much of their everyday life, environment and the way they and their mates live, grow, learn and communicate is almost unrecognisable from ours.

When I was fifteen, my biggest concern was whether I could sneak off to my room to record the Radio 1 Top 40 onto a cassette on a Sunday night.

Nowadays, at any one time my teens are usually communicating with eighteen people at once, via seven different platforms, on three different devices, from the privacy of their own rooms at any time of day or night.

This kind of techno change is the case for all generations. When the wireless was invented in the 1920s and people started listening to the World Service in their front rooms, 'experts' predicted the end of civilisation before *The Archers* ran its first emergency lambing story.

Ditto when televisions set up home in the corner of every house in the street.

'What will happen to us??' people despaired, watching a full twenty minutes of a twelve-inch television screen every other day. What happened to them was, of course, nothing much.

It was all fine; civilisation didn't end, nobody's brain

exploded, and we eventually worked out how to flick between the two available channels without having to get up off the sofa, and instead using an extendable aerial attached to a broom handle, thus allowing us to carry on eating bags of reconstituted corn starch, uninterrupted.

But the change in the world in the last twenty years really IS huge, and almost incomprehensibly so, even to us adults.

We had acres and hours of available PEACE, even when we were at war with our parents, and ourselves.

They, on the other hand, have noise, information, communication, bleeping, buzzing, pinging, copying, pasting, editing, cropping, faking, posting, sharing, deleting, panicking, doing, undoing, rushing, changing, worrying, melting.

They can access literally EVERYTHING THAT'S AVAILABLE ON THE WHOLE OF THE INTERNET.

Every piece of information.

Every photo.

Every video.

Every person.

At any time. Anywhere.

Even a two-year-old these days can do this.

We have no idea what they're doing in their rooms.

We have no idea what they're looking at on their mate's phone at school.

We have no idea who they communicate with.

We have no idea what they have seen, learned or done, online.

AND IT'S FUCKING TERRIFYING.

It should be.

It's like letting our kids run around on the M25 all day and all night, and wondering if they'll be hit by a car transporter.

Online life is probably the single biggest pant-shitter of parenting today, and nobody has any sure-fire way of dealing with it.

Because there IS no sure-fire way to deal with it.

It's an unknown. A constant risk. A moving goal post. A changing threat. An uncontrollable, invisible car transporter.

Worse, it's also a useful, essential part of their everyday life, so we *have* to engage with it.

It's constant dodgeball with grenades, and you don't know which one has had the pin pulled.

It's all hugely relaxing.

But it's possible. We CAN let them go online, and they CAN be perfectly safe.

Not every grenade goes off.

They CAN have both peace and phone pinging.

***

Here's what I know now, and wish I hadn't worried about then:

- However hard you try to instil rules and boundaries and systems and limits, you'll end up breaking most of them. And that's OK. We did, saw, ate and poked about with loads of things our parents didn't want us to, and we are (pretty much) OK. We learned about multiple orgasms in *Cosmo* and passed well-fingered porn mags to each other on the school bus, poured Bacardi into Coke cans at lunchtime, pierced our own ear lobes with rusty needles, and listened to music with lyrics so sexually explicit they were basically hardcore podcasts with a chorus – but despite all of this we didn't molest puppies or spit on grannies.

- Your kids will get around all your well-meaning parental blocks within minutes of you installing them. God knows how, but they will. There's always some nerd in the canteen who can de-code the Kremlin's iTunes account in seconds. Your 'foolproof parental safety blocks' will be dust in one lunch break. If they want to see the most awful, vile, abusive and disturbing kinds of porn they will find it. If they want to set up an online account and talk to men dressed up as superheroes and wanking into a Kinder egg, they will.
- They will see things they shouldn't. Just as we did.
- If you ban it in your house, they'll go get it in someone else's.
- They might have bullying issues on social media, at which point things can get extremely difficult, heated and upsetting. Exactly as happened when

we were kids, with playground bullying. If it happens, it can be ghastly. And it might happen. But it also might not.

- They CAN self-regulate. Really, they can. But every child is different. Some are shit at this, just as some adults are shit at not eating the entire packet of Maoams. Know your kids. Know their behaviour, moods and patterns. And do what THEY need you to do, regardless of how anyone else does it.
- Your online behaviour has a MASSIVE impact on theirs.
- Educate, educate, educate. That's the best we can do. Tell them everything you think they need to know about the good stuff out there, and the dangers. That way they can decide what's OK, and what's not. Because you won't always be there.

***

Here are some things you'll promise yourself you'll definitely do, and then definitely won't:

- No phones when they come home from school. NOPE.
- No phones after 8 p.m. NOPE.

- No phones at the table. Vaguely possible most of the time, but someone's always bleeps and gets checked. Usually mine.
- Detox as a family one evening a week. But... but... but TWITTER! No way.
- Detox on holiday. Are you trying to kill me?

And so on. Just do your best. Put it away for a wee while every day. Get your kids to do the same. Or don't. Do be concerned about it. Do keep vigilant. Do keep trying to protect them from the bad bits, and allow them to experience the good.

Just... DO YOUR FRICKIN' BEST, OK?! That's enough.

Party Time

Parties get a little… different, in the Middle Years.

Before I got all huffy and controlling about my kids' teenage parties, and labelled the lot of them as delinquent, drunken vandals, I decided to recall one of my own:

***

July 1990

My parents' house.

I am seventeen.

My parents have gone away for a long weekend, as parents used to do before Helicopter Parenting and Facebook were invented, after which 'going away for the weekend' became synonymous with 'letting 15,000 people we've never met come into our house, fill it with Class A drugs, and cut the hedge into a frieze of a Roman orgy'.

It's a shame, really. Kids miss out on a lot if they're never alone in a house full of booze and hedge-cutters.

According to the lists of all the things I have to remember that my mother has Blu-Tacked to every kitchen cupboard, 'things' include: not killing the houseplants; not killing the dog; not leaving lights on or wasting hot water or otherwise spending money unwisely; not leaving my dirty dishes in the sink because if we get burgled the police will come round and they might think that we live 'badly'; not forgetting to record Poirot, and The Archers too if I can get the tape player to work; not having a party or getting drunk, or both.

***

Friday night

11 p.m.

So far, all sixty or so of the people I've invited to my party seem to be having a good time, judging by the fact that they're singing loudly and dancing in the kitchen.

I am not so much drunk, as hammered. And possibly stoned, but I can't say for sure, on account of never having been stoned before so I'm not sure what being stoned is like, and also being so wasted on beer and Bacardi and Malibu and rum and wine and apple schnapps (WHO has apple schnapps in their house??) and Campari and gin, that I probably wouldn't notice if I were.

Technically, I'm not officially breaking any rules at all because, officially, I am technically only supposed to be in charge of 'things' over the weekend, and it's still only Friday night.

I'm not quite sure why so many people are in my house, but I *think it may have something to do with the fact that I went straight to the pub after school, drank half a shandy, stood on a table and invited everyone I know, and a fair few I don't, to my parents' house.*

Much alcohol is being consumed. A model of the Eiffel Tower is being poorly constructed out of pink ice cream wafers. All the ice cream in the freezer has already been eaten. Some of my dog's food is now being eaten, causing much mirth – though probably not to my dog, who I suspect is also stoned, given that she's been walking in a slow circle for three hours. Many lights are left on, and there's a chance that some hot water may have been used too, in a slightly wasteful way.

Sometime near midnight the garden becomes a disco, after John B manages to rig up a massive extension cable from the lounge and transport my dad's new speakers onto the lawn using a skateboard. Quite what happens next is still a mystery to everyone who was present, but whatever it is it results in Hugh pelting down the garden at full speed, not realising that there is a washing line across it, at nose height. While Hugh goes to the hospital to get his nose sewn back on, Chris demonstrates his handstand-while-balancing-a-bottle-of-rum-on-his-foot trick, falls into the flowerbed and lacerates his wrist on the broken bottle. While Chris goes to join Hugh in A&E, Lucy and Robert split up over a serious argument about whether Nirvana take themselves too seriously. It is judged that Nirvana would have approved of this break-up, and Lars Eriksson sings a song about it, called 'Serious Love Prob-

lems' in a strong Danish accent, while playing my brother's guitar. Which is weird, because my brother doesn't own a guitar. I think Clare is sick on the new patio around about this time, but I'm not sure, as it was around now that I passed out, wearing a colander as a hat.

The last thing I remember of that night is waking up with a mouth like the Sahara made of nails, reaching for the nearest glass of water, downing it in one, and then realising it was vodka.

And then passing out again.

***

Remember those kids' birthday parties we used to curse, in cold church halls that smelled of nappies, with inexplicably expensive, definitely dodgy 'entertainers' who turned up with a fake washing machine, one red sock and disturbingly stained trousers; tortuous hours playing party games with seventy-five screaming, objectionable kids you don't even like but had to invite because their parents live within shit-stirring distance and it's socially safer to just pay for another goddam balloon and slice of definitely-not-home-made birthday cake than face the bitching; necking as much booze as you can between rounds of pass-the-parcel-nobody-cares-about-anyway, and then mopping up several pints of wee after three wired little bastards got over-excited in the ball-pit?

While raising my oldest three children, I shelled out for

and endured the ear-splitting hell of nearly thirty of those birthday parties.

That's a LOT of wee in ball-pits.

But here's the thing: one day they stop. And become VERY different beasts.

They become 'gatherings'. 'Get-togethers'. 'Hang-outs'.

Piss-ups. And yes, let's face it, drug-ups.

Suddenly, dodgy kids' entertainers and a game of musical chairs seems very appealing.

It comes fast, it comes as a surprise, and it takes a bit of a shift of mind-set.

There are basically two options:

Clamp down, or loosen the fuck up.

Forbid it all, monitor them like a traffic warden with a hard-on in central London on a Bank Holiday just itching for that next ticket, or chill out and let them get on with doing things all teenagers do.

My strategy of coping with my kids doing all the things I worried about was to remember what I was doing at their age. After the panic had subsided, I then reminded myself that it's completely normal at their age, even important, to do things our bodies and minds would rather we didn't, to crash a car on a mini roundabout, to smoke things we found growing in a hedge, to put our hands and tongues and underwear where they've never been, wear colanders as hats and make a lot of mistakes.

We made it to adulthood perfectly well, thank you, with most of our teeth intact. Just not Hugh's nose.

Of course they'll push every boundary you can imagine, and rightly so: children who never rebel become mass murderers or drink bubble tea. Or both.

For the most part, teenage rebellion is pretty tame, and more annoying than dangerous or concerning: bedtimes get pushed ever later because they're sharing GIFs of people farting in amusing ways, phones are on when you've told them to switch them off, lies are told about homework and whose house they have been to, the smell of cigarette smoke is pathetically concealed beneath cheap perfume, love bites are passed off as a sudden intolerance to cheese.

The first teenage house parties my kids had were not so much scenes of carnage, smashed windows and multiple pregnancies, and more a case of deep-voiced, badly coordinated, galumphing boys sitting around talking to girls with slightly too much midriff on display, drinking cider out of plastic cups.

A couple of times some pubescent girl or other with burgeoning breasts, whom I last saw playing hide and seek in Year 2 wearing a Dora the Explorer backpack, threw up in one of my salad bowls, and an empty Alcopop was once found on the piano.

CALL THE POLICE.

It's fine. Very few children go from angel to full-blown narcotics dealer overnight.

To get into a panic about it is really unnecessary and unhelpful.

For now, it's enough just to adjust to the sudden realisation that the child who used to make Playdough sausages with you is now ready to do all the things you hazily remember doing at that age – and then try not to think about it. You'll only turn into a neurotic psycho-mum, listening at the door and throwing away all the matches.

Just remember the good side to all of this – one day soon your child will be able to buy YOU a round. And drive you home.

WIN.

Social Media Rules

Never tag your children in a post without checking – and then triple checking.

Ever.

That's pretty much it.

SOCIAL MEDIA SUGGESTIONS

Spying on their social media: no. The word 'spying' should be a hint, really.

Anyway, you can't, because they'll have five secret accounts you're not aware of.

Annual social media clear-outs: yes.

Kids befriend everyone on social media. Literally everyone and anyone. That guy at the bus stop? Yeah, he's seen your holiday snaps from France because you stupidly drank too much rosé and then tagged your daughter in one of the pics. And now bus-stop guy knows what you look like in a see-through bikini, and what your fifteen-year-old daughter looks like in hers. Awesome.

However popular your kids are, they don't need 2,596 friends. They really don't.

So, sit down together, and clear them out. That bitch in Year 8? Gone, baby, gone. That guy who looks like he'd sell you any drug you can't even name? Deleted.

Teachers? (TEACHERS?) Unfriended.

I did this annual clear-up with my kids, and I think it was possibly one of the most useful parenting things I've managed to date.

It also made me aware of how terrifyingly grown-up (read 'sexually self-exploiting to the max') most eleven-year-olds look on their social media.

JESUS. It's terrifying.

But it's best to be aware that this is what your children are seeing too, and might want to emulate.

Regular social media chats: definitely.

Using social media openly in front of your kids: yes.

Leading by example: yes, as long as it's only one example of quite a long list of options, and they choose a different one to me.

In general, I can safely say that I hope my kids will do everything entirely differently to me, and much better.

We're all just human and do it too much ourselves and shouldn't, so by all means preach, and then practise practising it, but assume you'll fail and then just be honest with your kids about how shit you're being and let's all try to have a social media time-out together, yes?

Good Cop, Bad (Mummy) Cop

Someone has to be Bad Cop.

From what I've observed, it's almost always Mum.

I wear my Bad Cop helmet with pride, irritation, weariness and a hope that one day they'll understand why someone had to say no computers after 9 p.m. and go and wash your hands before you eat and stop WhatsApping under your duvet and no telly until the biology essay is finished and no you can't wear that top in public and take your feet off the sofa NOW and no that little shit Josh can't come to play any more after he brought cigarettes to your birthday party and you just got a new phone so you don't need another one for years and no I am not paying for you to have your own Spotify account and no you can't have wine with dinner yet because we Don't Do That In Our Family and what about reading some STEINBECK OR WAUGH for once and broadening your frickin' literary horizons and yes you DO have to make your bed every morning because it's good for you and I said no chocolate in the lounge, and don't SLAM THAT DOOR it's coming off the hinge!!!

Someone has to be Bad Cop. And it was me.

I don't care; I look darned hot in a police helmet.

Independence

In 1992 I went on a Gapyah, and saved up enough money working as a waitress/piano teacher/ice cream café manager to go around the world for six months with a backpack bigger than I was.

So off I went.

Seventeen years old. Struggling since school days with bulimia and anorexia and a crippling lack of self-confidence but, weirdly, also a huge inner strength and belief in myself and new-found happiness to be DOING MY OWN THING at long, long last.

Anyway. While I was away travelling, my parents wrote me airmail letters every so often, which I collected every month or two at one post office or other, in Singapore or Sydney or Somewhere.

I sent some postcards home, when I remembered, or had enough change from the last beer.

And everything was fine.

No Facebook posts.

No WhatsApp checking.

No panicking or terror or calls in the night because, darling, I've not heard ANYTHING from you for THREE HOURS.

Just me, alone, travelling around the world, and checking in every so often.

It was bliss.

Twenty years later, when my daughters went on their first Airbnb trips I tried to remember those sweaty post office queues to collect the letters I still have in my attic, and the freedom I had to just GO – what it taught me about life, people, myself, the world, and wearing more effective deodorant.

And I let them go. I didn't call, check their Instagram or message them constantly.

They texted to say they'd arrived, and we (mostly) had evening texts to say all was OK.

And that was that. And it was OK.

I think we really owe them that freedom, and, hard as it is, to back the hell off and let them have a go at messing it up on their own.

BIG Choices

'Cheese'n'onion or plain?'

This, along with 'now then, shall I eat this piece of snot, or roll it and flick it at my sister?' is pretty much the hardest decision of our kids' lives until they are twelve.

AND THEN…

It suddenly gets all woooaaaahhhhhhh.

GCSE choices.

Extracurricular choices.

A-level choices.

University choices.

Will they even go to university? If so, where, why, how?

Career options.

Financial questions.

Drugs or no drugs?

Relationship dilemmas and decisions.

Weekend job or school band practice?

Gap year or no gap year?

Live with Mum or live with Dad? (Yes, this is a question for a lot of teens, and it isn't an easy one.)

Study further or get a job?

Etc.

The choices and decisions get huge.

The big cheese'n'onion debate is suddenly replaced by:

Engineering or architecture?

Study or job?

These are questions that actually, like… AFFECT THEIR LIFE.

The good news is that they are, largely, not terminal.

Life is long, our kids will change their minds, and if they choose history instead of maths, it's likely nobody will die as a result.

Everything can seem so terrifying and consequential.

In fact, it all works out somehow in the end. They eventually find something they like doing, and, if they don't, they can change. If they're in The Class With All The Shitty Horrible Kids, they muddle through and often find good mates at extracurricular classes instead. If the choice of schools available to you are Not The Schools You Dreamed Of, they generally survive and it's just a different experience to the one we maybe expected for them. And maybe even a better one. Shitting bricks or getting angry doesn't help much. Having a good, supportive atmosphere at home does.

I've known kids change GCSE options within weeks of starting, change university courses halfway through, drop out of a chemistry degree to do a one-year conversion course in art and design, and love it.

It's all OK. They'll be OK. I'm forty-five and I don't know what I want to do when I grow up yet. (I'll always have the cheese'n'onion, in case we ever find ourselves in the pub together. Cheers.)

Mental Health

SURPRISE ANNOUNCEMENT:

The Middle Years are generally pretty stressful for kids.

And stress can cause mental health wobbles.

Boom.

There are still, amazingly, quite a few people out there who use the old 'snowflake' line and tell us how life has always been tough, and it was harder back in My Day and we were raised on string and smacking, and what the hell is WRONG with kids these days, I'll tell you what, they're on their phones all day long, plugged into the intersphere and social chat-sites and All The Porn, and there's no discipline or manners or bloody good old FRESH AIR and they're allowed to rule the roost like little Buddhas by their awful parents when really they need a good hiding and some GODDAM MANNERS, and all this talk about anxiety this and depression that is all just a load of WISHYWASHY-CODSWALLOP.

There are those people.

Those people are, to use the correct, academic terminology, morons. They're also often fairly fucked up themselves, possibly thanks to all that string and smacking, but they don't know it, or couldn't admit it if they tried, and anyway they don't care because they bought a house in 1963 for 85p which is now worth £2.5 million, from which they can comfortably slag off the younger generation who will never be able to afford so much as a brick to lob through the windows of the twats.

To them I say: you snowflake me; I'll fucking avalanche you, mate.

Let's not be those people. Let's be non-morons and understand that life is bloody hard for our kids growing up now, and much harder in many ways than it was for us, or our parents.

I'm a huge advocate of mental health care and understanding, and believe it's a little more helpful to open our eyes to the idea that our kids MIGHT have some mental health issues at some point, and in fact, because they are human beings, it's not wholly unlikely.

And it's best to know this and be there to HELP when it happens.

Basically, the Middle Years are hard for kids. You remember being fourteen, right?

They grow a lot.

They change a lot.

Body stuff is tough.

School is tough.

Friendships are tough.

Family issues can be tough.

Now throw in social media, the knowledge that you'll probably never get a job even if you DO ace your A-levels and will probably be homeless until you're thirty-five, and you're REALLY talking EPIC TOUGH.

The rates of anxiety, eating disorders, depression, self-harm etc. etc. etc. etc. ET FUCKING CETERA in young people is absolutely goddam horrendous. Actual. Fact.

***

Things to maybe NOT do:

Ignore it all because your kids will be fine.

Tell them to pull all the socks up and just Be Better.

Ignore it all.

Shout.

Ignore it all.

***

Things to maybe bear in mind:

Mental health problems can be very hard to spot. Anorexia is quite easy, obviously, but bulimia, addictions, self-harm, anxiety, depression and others, can go undetected for a LONG time.

Mental health problems can come and go, wax and wane, and have good periods and bad periods. That's normal and expected. It's the same for adults.

Mental health problems can be reduced by calm, understanding, support and love. The key word here is CALM. Oh, and love. And understanding. And support. Yeah, so all of it really.

Observation is your friend. If your kids seem to just... change, in their moods, behaviour, general... wellness, or unwellness, keep an eye on it.

It might be nothing. But it might be something.

Family stresses can be picked up way more than we might think, and manifest in lots of ways.

You might not be the person to deal with your own child's mental health wobbles. Some kids find it impossible to talk to their parents about it. In fact, many do. That's OK.

There are loads of places to get help – school counsellors, teachers, your GP, local groups, reading about it together, talking about it. At least one of my children went to the school counsellor or their GP when things at home were really difficult. They needed to talk to someone else, and almost certainly just shout, scream and massively slag the pair of us SHITTY BASTARD DISASTER PARENTS off. That's totally natural, and it helped a lot.

Don't get angry. Even when the situation is driving you to the edge of worry and frustration. Don't get angry. It doesn't help*.

Don't blame yourself*.

Don't blame yourself.

It might pass. It might not. But educating yourselves on

how to manage it, and how to do it as a family, calmly, is key.

Don't blame yourself.

*unless you are one of the aforementioned morons, in which case please do blame yourself for the rest of your sad, miserable days, because it is hugely your fault, and I hope you know it.

And hey, guess what? Your kids might have NO mental health issues at all.

Many of them get through it all perfectly well without any major mental OMGGGGGGGGGG whatsoever. It's just another thing to add to the list of things that CAN happen, and to know what to do if it does.

Sex Stuff

I lost my virginity in 1991 on a slab of moss-covered concrete next to a storage shed on the football field at my school.

I was sixteen.

He was Spanish.

He couldn't speak English, but managed to convey, 'I put my penis in your bagina?' using sign language.

(It's just occurred to me that he may have been offering to clean out my clarinet by ramming a small piece of paper into the end of it using his finger as a prodding stick, and I accidentally shagged him. Not a bad result, mate, especially considering I didn't even play the clarinet.)

Anyway. It happened.

It hurt.

To take my mind off the pain and awkwardness, I counted the number of hockey sticks I could see through the shed window.

I counted twelve. He scored.

We almost never spoke again, but given that we'd never spoken before this was no great loss to our relationship.

The bloody job was done.

I could now proceed into the Next Stage of my life, knowing that my hymen was officially dust, and I was Officially A Little Bit Cool.

ARE YOU HAVING SEX YET, DARLING?

Top of the List of Questions I Really Want to Ask My Kids, that one.

There are only three possible answers:

'Yes', 'No' and 'Look, I'M TRYING TO, OK?!'

(There is a fourth answer, involving prolonged silence and much floor-staring. Pray you don't get that one.)

The Sex Question crosses all of our minds at some point, especially when our kids start disappearing into their rooms for hours, emerging with cheeks the colour of an English tourist after a week in Marbella, and desperately trying to shove their stained bed sheets into the wash.

Inquisitive Eyebrow and Head-Tilt Dances can occur for a few months, followed by open, honest conversations about it all:

'...?'

'?...'

'...?...'

'...!...'

'...'

Glad we talked, honey.

According to the Daily Rant, all children nowadays are poking their genitals in each other's faces and swapping STIs when they're still in primary school. This kind of balanced reporting has had the fabulous knock-on effect of throwing millions of parents into a sex panic, demanding that the National Curriculum include lessons on cunnilingus in Key Stage 1, and hiding condoms under the cheese strings in their packed lunch. Though the latter may be more of a subliminal hint for Ralph's hot dad, if we're honest.

The truth is more… that they're not doing all that. They are more likely to be sending their mates triple-chin selfies, or flicking bogies at each other, like all happy kids do.

The age at which sexual shenanigans starts varies enormously, as it always has.

I had no interest in boys whatsoever until I was fifteen. Other girls in my class were already humping their way through the Sixth Form when they were twelve.

One day it dawned on me that 'getting off' with people was the currency by which Coolness was measured, and I was absolutely SKINT. So, I doused myself with The Body Shop's 'White Musk and Panic', and went out there to GET ME SOME.

Tongues, hands, trouser zips and acne blurred into a mess of greasy, hormonal bewilderment and disappointment.

That's how it happened for most of us. And still does.

There's no 'norm' or 'expected age'. It's largely about personality, age of sexual development, circumstances and a thick semeny dollop of luck – good or bad.

Far from being a lost generation of sexual deviants, addicted to online porn and sexting, almost the opposite has happened: the Coolness Currency has changed, there's been a crash in the groping market, and the fellatio index has dropped to record lows. Teenage pregnancies are down, and sexual health is actually far better than in previous years.

Why?

Because it's now FAR cooler to be yourself.

To stand up for what you feel is right for you.

Kids these days are encouraged FAR more than we ever were, in our 'don't talk about it and it'll be OK, luv', to read about sex and relationships, know about it, educate themselves about it, talk about it and be confident about it.

They're also educated and encouraged to understand something that was as lacking as a condom at a bus-stop fumble in my day: RESPECT.

I think this is the single most important thing we can teach our children about sex – and indeed about all aspects of relationships with all people.

Respect for themselves, and respect for others.

We were taught about the ins and outs, the biology, chemistry and physics of sex.

But rarely – unless you had impressively aware, engaged parents – about the emotional, personal and goddam USEFUL stuff.

I've done Sex Stuff Things that sometimes make me SCREAM when I realise how little I wanted to do them, but felt unable to say no to. What I put myself through in order to fulfil someone else's desires, and under pressure to please.

I wish I'd known better.

I wish I'd been more confident to say no.

I wish I'd been encouraged to be strong enough to know that was OK.

I wish I'd been more respectful towards myself, and my boundaries.

I wish a lot of it had never happened, even now, in my forties.

And I hope I've got children who will never have to write the above, at any age.

NOT UNDER MY ROOF

When I was a teenager, all sexual activities were conducted out of the house.

The world became a treasure hunt for dark corners, in which horny, confused, frightened teens tried to connect parts of their own anatomy to parts of other teenagers' anatomies, preferably without getting their braces stuck together and requiring the fire brigade to separate them.

Parks, bus shelters, bushes, public toilets, abandoned garages, phone boxes – you name it, we fumbled about in them.

The school bus was nothing short of a mobile sex den.

But even when I finally had a boyfriend with whom I could bravely hold hands in public, I would never, EVER, have asked my parents if he could stay the night.

I could have asked, but I think it's fair to say the next Ice Age would have commenced immediately.

When it came to my turn as a mum, and my daughters started to have boyfriends and bring them home, I took the clear, strong, responsible stance of... buckling like wet cardboard and saying absolutely nothing about it.

I didn't say no, I barely discussed rules, or boundaries, or made any kind of attempt to have any authority or Parentyness about it at all.

It just sort of happened.

I honestly don't have any better explanation for this occurrence, other than... it occurred.

Maybe I was too busy working or Hoovering or worrying about my greying hair to register it properly until it was too late, and the slippery slope had already been unstoppably slipped down; maybe I was too tired by work and life and admin to have had the strength left to argue. Maybe I didn't want to be Bad Cop this one time.

Or maybe I just trusted my kids enough to know it would be OK.

Whatever the reason, it happened.

I remember feeling I'd properly ballsed-up something important, and had in some way been a Shit, Irresponsible Parent and cocked up a Vital Moment in a child's life.

But you know what happened?

Nothing.

NOBODY DIED.

Nobody cried.

Nobody got syphilis.

And they stayed in good, strong, stable and happy relationships for ages.

Win.

Lie-ins

****GOLDEN NEWS KLAXON****

Lie-ins. Happen.

THEY ACTUALLY HAPPEN.

One day you wake up and it's not 5.30 a.m.

Or 6.47 a.m.

Or even 7.50 a.m.

It's… 9 a.m.

And you just woke up. By yourself. Naturally.

Without a board book, an elbow or a milk bottle being rammed into your eye socket.

Without a fight breaking out from next door over whose turn it is with the plastic mobile phone that's fucking broken anyway so who CARES, guys?!

Without the buzz of an alarm, the panic of missed football practice, the cry of a child with colic/toothache/sickness/chicken pox/nits/nightmares/too light/too dark/too on their own/too not on their own.

Just a sleep. And then an awake.

Just like that.

And slowly, this becomes the norm, until one day... things actually reverse.

They start sleeping longer than you.

AND THEN YOU HAVE TO START WAKING THEM UP.

The first time this happened was one of the most glorious moments of my parenting life.

That first day I went into their bedroom, swooshed open the curtains to dazzle them in 10 billion rays of blinding sunlight and told my peacefully sleeping child to WAKE UP AND GET THE HECK UP NOW. Up, up, up you get! C'mon! Let's go!

They hated me. They looked pained, exhausted and pissed off.

It was fantastic.

Go in there. Wake those bastards up. An hour earlier than you need to. Two, if you can be bothered.

Smack 'em in the eye socket with a hardback copy of *Lès Misérables.*

THIS IS PAYBACK. And it tastes divine.

Clothing Rebellion

As our kids get older, we enter the terrifying realm of Very Important Moments In Their Emotional Development That They Will Never Forget And Will Always Hold Us Accountable For And Consequently We Must Not Under Any Circumstances Cock Up.

One such 'key moment' is 'Self-Expression Through Clothing'.

You know, that day when your once-angelic child decides it's time to 'find their true self' through sartorial experimentation, and starts buying their own clothes – regardless of whether they suit them, fit them, are in any way practical, affordable, or make them look like a cheap, disease-ridden, card-carrying, loose-lipped whore.

Say.

Here's how it went for me:

My daughter got some money for her twelfth birthday.

She went to a shop that rhymes with Frymark.

She spent said birthday money on some items of clothing, and came home, proudly waving a giant paper bag.

I decided to play it cool and wait and see what she had purchased.

Perhaps she had chosen something lovely. Perhaps she had 'found her true self' in a nice, sensible pair of trousers and a plain T-shirt, which wouldn't shrink too badly in the wash and was economically unisex enough to be passed down to her little brother one day.

Perhaps she'd managed to find a jumper that didn't have 'Kiss My Baby Ass, Bitch' emblazoned across it.

Perhaps I was going to manage not to screw up this defining moment.

She disappeared into her bedroom, excitedly.

Ten minutes passed, nervously.

Much crashing was heard from behind the door, ominously.

I chewed the skin on the inside of my lip, paced up and down the landing, swore and removed a tiny plastic sword from the underside of my foot.

I began to wonder how it could possibly take so long to put clothes onto such a small person, and which came to a total of £10.

And then…

THERE SHE WAS!

Emerging triumphantly from her room, she did a little twirl on the landing.

Somewhere in the world, a flock of beautiful birds flew head-on into an aeroplane propeller.

There, attached to my beautiful, sweet little girl were, in no particular order of eye-watering horror:

- fluorescent-yellow, ripped fishnet gloves;
- a skirt made of a strip of purple Lycra, tightly stretched to cover most of her buttocks, but sadly not all of her crotch;
- a slouchy black vest adorned with a picture of what looked a bit like female genitalia, but might have been a mouth after a botched collagen injection;
- three inches of pubescent side-boob;
- an assortment of chunky, bubblegum-pink plastic bangles;
- three silver chains dangling to pubescent nipple height, one with a diamanté 'BABE' pendant;
- a three-inch wide, pink satin, leopard-print hair band;
- the unmistakable scent of the Death of Innocence.

She waited expectantly, still twirling, but now in a disturbingly provocative, 'I'm going to twerk your mind into agreeing with my choices' kind of way.

It was Rihanna meets Heidi, with visible camel toe and a dash of potential chlamydia.

I knew that I had three crucial seconds in which to say something complimentary, supportive, confidence-building and kind. Or, at the very least, to make a face that might convey some of this.

'Honey,' I said, choking on my own spit, 'you look like a prostitute. And not the expensive kind. You are NOT going out dressed like that. Go and take it all off.'

Someone screamed.

A door slammed.

I heard the words 'hate', 'I' and 'you', though not necessarily in that order.

I decided now wasn't the moment for the 'Do Not Swear At Your Mother!' conversation, and instead spent an hour banging my forehead onto the carpet, letting out a low, regretful moan.

All I'd had to do was lie and tell her she looked lovely.

But I'd messed it up completely.

I learned from this that there is never a good moment to criticise one's child's choice of clothing.

It just hurts them, and hurts us.

They have to learn what looks fucking horrendous for themselves.

Generation Clean

There's something wrong with teenagers these days: by far the majority of them, are... GOOD.

Horribly good.

Annoyingly good.

Disturbingly good.

Today's teens are less likely to drink, smoke and take drugs than their predecessors, making them the most sensible, healthy and fresh-smelling generation for a decade.

I'm probably supposed to rejoice and crack open a can of sparkling mineral water to toast this announcement of Good Behaviour, and the death of the teenage hangover.

But all I can think is... GUYS, SERIOUSLY?

Go and push some boundaries, will you?

Go and scratch your name into a park bench with your teeth.

Ruffle your greasy Teenfeathers, get them burned a bit, provoke your parents into an early breakdown, back-comb your hair into oblivion, finger a stained copy of *Razzle* and make some mistakes. Please?

Stop sitting in your room drinking goji berry juice and doing fitness workouts on YouTube.

Stop expressing your personality by following carefully curated, impossibly dull, pointless Instagram accounts, measuring your self-worth in 'likes', and socialising with the whole world, alone in your room.

I'd far rather you learned to down the occasional can of Heineken with your mates in the park, than spent two hours taking posed selfies of yourself in your bedroom with the doors closed.

I'd rather you threw up at a friend's party and learned about your own alcohol tolerance, that Campari and Special Brew don't mix and that hangovers are fuckin' awful, than spent an hour staring at edited pictures of Cara Delevingne online, and loathing yourself.

I'd rather you had a smoke and snogged some guy in Year 11 you don't even like, than sat alone in Cyberspace with people you don't know, whilst working out the amount of omega-3 in your smoothie.

I don't *want* my kids to smoke, drink or take drugs.

Really, I don't. At all.

But I think I'd rather see them doing some old-fashioned Teenage Bad Things, getting down and dirty and learning first-hand about people and Life, than watch them grow up living 'cleanly' in a disturbingly manufactured, controlled but uncontrollable world they feel they can create for themselves, while having no clue how to deal with the hard knocks and bumps of real life because they've lived so little of it that they don't understand how it works.

That's a danger, to both physical and mental health, that I don't think we fully understand yet. And one we should be very cautious of.

See you all down the disco on Friday, then. Beers on me. Tongues optional.

Anger

Older kids can get angry.

Very angry.

And no, not just the boys. Girls can get SUPER RAGEY too.

(So can their mums…)

We're not great at talking about, understanding or dealing with anger, in my opinion, and we fear teenage rage as if it's The Beast Gone Mad, and needs containing or 'treating'.

This is all deeply unhelpful.

When a toddler gets angry, we call it a tantrum.

But when a teenager has 'tantrums' everyone goes into a massive parenting panic and assumes they have serious behavioural issues, psychological problems or have been brainwashed by some Anger Cult online and need emergency counselling and perhaps some Ritalin and electric shock therapy thrown in for good measure.

In most cases they don't. They're just Being Normal Older Kids.

Teenagers are a shuffling nuclear bomb of hormones, growing pains, emotional confusion, physical change, YouTube overload and horniness, just waiting to explode.

And amazingly, once in a while – KABOOM!

Ex-plo-sion. Things are thrown. Things are smashed. Things are broken. Things are shouted. Things are ripped. Things are regretted.

Let it boom, let it boom, let it boom.

Let that pressure get out.

Most people calm down after a good shout, and any mess can be cleared, sorted and mended.

Anger, rages, strops and tantrums are normal between the ages of about eight and eighteen.

Not long then…

This is all up to a point though, obviously.

Shouting once in a while: cool.

Daily rage for weeks… not so cool, and maybe a wee chat is in order. Calmly… but yeah. Definitely have a chat and see what's up, pussycat. Because something seems to be.

NOTE: this 'chat' thing can take AGES. Days, weeks of patience and observation, suggestions and clearly indicated open doors for 'want a chat, honey?'

Don't give up.

They need you to not give up.

H is for Hormones. BECAUSE IT JUST IS, OK???

Hormones are shit.

Hormones make us angry.

Hormones make us sad. And confused. And irritable. And irrational. And happy. And moody. And spotty. And fat. And mad. And forgetful. And tired. And forgetful.

Basically, they sometimes make us behave and feel and BE not at all in a way we would like to, or mean to, or are even aware of.

Unfortunately, their shitness isn't reserved for us; they do all of these things to our children too.

Often, just at a time when we are struggling with hormonal changes of our own, which are making us confused and hot and cold and fat and irritable and angry and sad and... IS THAT A HOT FLUSH??

This can make living in a house together a bit like being in a war zone in a hurricane in a heatwave, in a village of mad people.

Everyone is hormonal.

The cat is hormonal.

The air is hormonal.

Some people's kids get hormonally edgyyyyyyyy at twelve.

For others it's more like fourteen, or even older. There are more factors involved in the onset of puberty than anyone can ever fathom, and most of it is almost certainly our fault in some inexplicable, inexcusable way. It just is what it is, and Nature does her hormoney thing when she's ready.

Oh, and that thing about synchronising cycles? Yeah, never noticed it, to be honest. At least three of the five of us in our family were hormonally fucked at any one time, for about fifteen years. Periods started, beards grew, shoulders doubled in breadth, breasts swelled, acne arrived, chests got deeper, voices dropped, thighs got all varieties of wrong, sleeps got disrupted, showers got longer, smells got weirder, arguments got fiercer, tears came, panics started, and so it went on and on.

It's all a bit more manageable if you try to remember this: the moody shit-storm is something they can't control.

And neither can you.

Hugs work.

Shouting doesn't.

Crying is good, if it eventually stops.

Talking is essential.

Cuddles are the best.

Tolerance is advised.

Patience is key.

Going for long walks is life-saving.

They don't like it any more than you do.

You're all in the hormonal soup together. Keep swimming gently and see what the land looks like when you get to the far side.

The Clothing Police

If I ever get run over by the number 7 bus on the way to work, it's a pretty safe bet that the last words I'd have heard my children sigh at me that morning would have been:

'Mum, what are you… wearing?'

Somewhere around my fortieth birthday, my clothing style – or lack of it – became a free-for-all for the kind of skin-peeling criticism usually reserved for the *Daily Mail*'s online bitch-fest comment section.

This didn't do much to soothe my growing and uncomfortable awareness that I was suddenly teetering along that delicate style-high-wire between mutton-dressed-as-lamb and Gelatinous Frump.

(I feel there's quite a big market for this complicated style stage, so I've bought www.muttonfrump.com just in case I decide to go for it.)

Whether my clothes were actually nice or not was immaterial in my children's eyes; to them, my entire wardrobe was a sartorial atom bomb:

my jeans were too short/long/cool/black/tight/loose/wrong;

my shirts were too boring/bright/revealing/dull/loose/not right with that skirt;

my shoes were too young/old/comfy/sexy;

my jumpers were too jumperish;

my socks were too… why are you WEARING SOCKS, MUM??

Whatever I wore, my clothing represented the epitome of Uncool and Social Pain, with a sprinkling of Incontinent Geriatric thrown in, and there was nothing I could do to change this.

It took a while, but I did finally relent and accept that the time had come to see Topshop as a nostalgic trip down memory lane, not a shopping destination – except for my teenagers.

The only exception to my fashion mauling was on the very rare occasions when my daughters wanted to borrow something of *mine*, at which point everything I owned became a free-for-all, my wardrobe was ransacked, and I never saw any of my thick black tights again.

I call this shameless double standards. They call it 'OH MY GOD I LOVE THIS! And you never wear it anyway so it's like recycling, really. AND I've helped to clear out your cupboard a bit, see?'

NOTE: the moment you see your pubescent daughter wearing an item of your clothing, you know you will never EVER be able to wear it again. She will wear it with such ease, natural flair and a slightly disturbing burgeoning sexuality, that next to her you can only look like a mutant toad in a sausage skin, if you try it on.

Never let your daughters wear your favourite items of clothing. You have been duly warned.

Daughters and Sons

I have three daughters, and one son.

(That's a LOT of oestrogen for one lad to be dealing with, poor chap. Anyway.)

The Middle Years threw a few unexpected thoughts and issues about both sexes at me, in parenting terms, that I wish I'd known.

Here are a few.

Ladies first:

DAUGHTERS

I'd always wanted two daughters because a) I am greedy and it's just want, want, want with me, and b) that way they could have what I yearned for when I was growing up, and might have made me a kinder person, or less weird or difficult or self-loathing and more confident with my hair, or something:

I yearned for a SISTER.

(I suspect this yearning for a sister is largely because I don't have one and therefore don't know how annoying they are, but anyway. I want one, I don't have one, so I made some for my kids instead. YOU ARE ALL SO WELCOME, my loves.)

As extraordinary luck would have it my body has kindly made me three babies with two X chromosomes in the bit where their fiddly bits are decided.

Two X chromosomes are the biological recipe for boobs and a fanny, and, as all geneticists know, the Xs stand for Xtremely lovely and Xtremely complicated.

Men have an X and a Y, which stand for 'Xactly When Can I Have Sex Again?' and 'Y Don't You Move The Mug Yourself If You're So Bothered About It.' We'll get to them later.

I've learned lots from my daughters.

I've learned about myself as a mother, a daughter, a friend and a person.

I've learned that if you leave the bathroom unmanned for five minutes, Little Hands will find their way into your cupboard and help themselves to all the nice stuff. Especially the most expensive eye cream an overdraft can buy.

And I've learned that girls are very, very, very, very, very, very, very complicated. Especially in the Middle Years.

Baby girls are a cinch. First of all, when you're changing their nappy they don't wee in your face when you're standing two feet away. That's pretty handy.

Actually, that's about all. THAT is the sum total of why baby girls are easier than baby boys. But it's a good one so WELL DONE, little ladies.

Around the age of five or so most little girls start preparing for their first relationships, by becoming bossy, hyper-controlling, argumentative, sulky and intolerant of everything that doesn't fit into Their Plan, and organising things in their own Mini Dictatorship way, which is the only CORRECT WAY.

This exhausting phase lasts about ten years.

Then come the Middle Years, and FRIENDSHIP GROUPS.

Christ.

When Miss Hannigan sings, 'I'm done with little girls!' in the musical *Annie*, I always feel like taking her aside and saying...

'Oh yeah? Just you WAIT until they're older, sweetheart.'

What IS it with females and bloody friendship groups?? The number of times my daughters and their mates have had major, emotionally shattering 'friendship issues' is more than I've accidentally plucked my eyelashes out while turning to stop one of them hurling a phone out of the window during an emotionally exhausting friendship issue.

Week in, week out for years we had tears and traumas as one 'friend' or other actually turned out to be a fuckingwhorebitchcow, and the older they got, the more fuckingwhorebitchcows there seemed to be. Until they weren't again, because just when you cotton on to who is currently a fuckingwhorebitchcow, and reference them this way in some kind of mum–daughter solidarity, it NOW turns out they're REALLY NICE, MUM, and it was just a Thing.

My bad. I clearly missed the update since this morning's top story.

In the Middle Years, the deadly undercurrent of friendship-group fireworks can suck the whole family down with it if someone foolishly goes to school with the wrong brand of shoelaces or fewer than 800 likes on BestieSnap or MingeGossip, or whatever the hot platform is this week.

Arguments no longer take place in the playground. They spread, multiply and infect virally via Insta stories and WhatsAaaaaaaaaarghghghghgghp.

And they change with the wind.

I feel really sorry for them, I genuinely do. I mean, honestly, WHO would want to be a teenager these days? They live under the kind of social (and academic/life) pressure we can't even begin to imagine. The worst that could happen when I was fifteen was not knowing how to pretend to inhale without the thick, white, clearly-not-inhaled-at-all smoke tumbling out of the corners of your mouth like a duvet, as you slowly choked and coughed into a coma, nodding nonchalantly.

People took the piss out of you. Bullying happened. It wasn't nice, but it was teenagehood. Friends were made and lost. But that was that.

Teenage girls don't have friends any more; they have social enablers. They don't bitch; they destroy. They don't have a close friend; they have Besties, very publicly. They even have 'BFFL's.

For LIFE? No pressure, then.

It's almost a parenting requirement now to have a degree in social media and communication, just to know what our kids are talking about, let alone how to help or advise them when things get a bit bitch-for-bitch out there.

Social media is the ideal tool for teenage girls, as it allows bitching, back-stabbing and glorified self-promotion on a scale and at a speed that could only have been dreamed about by the classroom bullies of old.

It's basically a massive catfight waiting to happen. And sometimes it does.

Brace yerselves.

Be there for them.

Be that sister we all wish we had.

Be the mother you'd like to be for them.

Even when they are being a fuckingwhorebitchcow to you.

It's that X chromosome again, doing its thing.

SONS

From what I've observed over twenty years of parenting, and, if you'll forgive me for generalising hugely, here is what I've concluded about boys, and friendship stuff:

They're not remotely fussed about friendship groups, 'besties' and cliques. They just kick balls about, sometimes punch each other because apparently that's OK and fun, and just occasionally they'll suddenly get really chatty and sociable, and will reply to their mate's three-week-old WhatsApp message with something deep and meaningful, like 'Lolz'.

Sometimes they don't like each other for a few days. Then they do again. And that's all you'll ever hear about it.

Sons can be the cuddliest, gentlest, loveliest, calmest, most thoughtful, kind, balanced, sensible, non-judgemental, life-affirming, sense-talking, love-giving, dinner-cooking, shit-sorting people in your life. And when they're done, off they go to play again. No further words or complications needed. Easy as that. And it's LOVELY.

(If you think I've given just a TAD more space here to girls and friendship issues than boys, then congratulations – you are quite right. And I think that says it all.)

***

SIDE-NOTE:

When daughters want something, they'll ask their dad.

EVERY time, and especially if we've just said no. Twice.

They're smart enough to know that there's a solid 98 per cent chance he'll say yes.

Firstly, because this way he's undermining any shred of authority we might have left, and he finds this satisfyingly annoying.

But mainly because she's his Little Girl. Even when she's thirty-seven.

It's maddening, but just how it is.

We get to share tampons. They get to share the Kettle Chips you JUST SAID she can't have.

Deal with it and move on.

THE MOTHER–DAUGHTER STING

If you're a woman and you have a daughter, I'm gonna just tell you this now so if this happens to you don't think you've failed in any way or have a Disastrous Relationship With Your Daughter.

Mums and daughters don't always get on like the bestest best mates ever.

Sometimes we do, and it's lovely.

But sometimes, we CLASH.

HUGELY.

And it burns. Deep.

Generally it doesn't kick in until the Middle Years, when daughters can get so goddam sensitive and narky towards us that we need to ask Siri to please go and check for us if she's nearly out of the shower, because if we so much as cough quietly near the door we'll get a nuclear explosion of 'I'LL COME OUT WHEN I'M READY OK?! Jesus. Privacy much??!' from the other side.

This is bad enough. But I found it was all made much worse by the pretty loud noises Out There on social media, in magazines and so on, of close mum–daughter bonds, love and laughs, that I felt I wasn't getting a whole lot of in-between the sighs, if I'm honest.

There's so much put out there about all these amazing, happy, close, mutually supportive 'special connections' between mums and daughters, with spa weekends, twinning (GOD NO), shopping trips together, shared hairdresser appointments, nail bar sessions, dual gym membership, double dates.

BLOODY HELL the amount of amaaaaaazing fun and closeness everyone is having with their daughters, it's a wonder anyone else gets a look-in.

So listen here:

If you're at home and your once lovely little girl-child is now a sulky, argumentative little cow-teenager who disagrees with EVERYTHING you do, say, want, think and feel, how you breathe, walk, dress, move, drink your coffee, sit at the table, touch your hair, chew your food and talk, what you watch, read, listen to, like and wear… just know that this is…

FAR MORE NORMAL than massive weekend love-ins in a spa.

My advice, for what it's worth, is this: don't clash back.

There's no point, and it goes nowhere good.

They don't even know why they're being shitty, so trying to out-shit them, or shout it down, criticise, berate, weep or abandon, is pointless.

And probably just turns the prickle-dial up to nearer eleven.

Keep calm and carry on being sighed at.

Be lovely. Be patient. Be nice. Even when they're being horrendous.

Take it, as far as you can.

When you can't take it, and you scream at them, because FFS you're human and we all have limits, just do the right thing and apologise afterwards.

Even if you are TOTALLY in the right.

They are confused. So are you.

They are hormonal. So are you.

They are struggling with the world. So are you.

They are stressed. So are you.

They probably just want a hug. So do you.

Say What?

Me: Hey, sweetie, what are you up to?

Five-year-old child: I'm making a fort and inside it's all magic and it means things can FLY and also be so quiet you can't hear it and I'm going to make a HOUSE in the fort and keep my special dust in it that makes me invisible but ONLY my horse can see me so we can go out and find special secret things and NOBODY will see us because when I sit on the horse SHE goes all invisible TOO so we can fly ANYWHERE and eat all the cake and strawberries and sausages and go anywhere we want and see everything and all the people and find things and when we get back we can share all our secrets that we collected and put them in a big box where they can stay forever.

***

Me: Hey, sweetie, what you up to, honey?

Fourteen-year-old child: '–'

***

So there's… that.

Only for about five years.

Enjoy the silence.

Or try Messenger. You might actually get an answer.

***

After a few years of communication (and more often miscommunication) via monosyllabic grunting, texts and emojis, I found things suddenly changed when they were sixteen or so and we started having the most amazing, interesting, open chats.

And that continues to this day – with occasional periods of sulky, moody silence, which I'd say just shows them all to be human and normal.

I've lost the flying horses and boxes full of magic secrets, but gained hours of talk about the news, films I've not seen, jumpsuits I definitely need to buy and special deals on facepacks at Boots. So, it's all good.

Teenagers Are Awful

They are rude.
They have no manners.
They are irritable and moody.
They won't want to talk to their parents any more.
They only want money and food.
They have eating problems and anger issues.
They sulk in their rooms.
They are THE WORST THINGS EVER.

***

Also worth considering:
Teenagers are amazing.
They have fantastic ideas.
They are kind.
They give good talk.
They give good listen.
They are fun.
They're great to travel with.

They can come to the cinema with us to see films we might actually want to see.

They are full of ideas and creativity.

They are fascinating.

They are challenging.

They are beautiful.

They are endlessly surprising.

They are needy of us, still.

They are vulnerable.

They are strong.

They are weak.

They are supremely confident, and utterly terrified.

They need guidance, and freedom.

They are argumentative – and that's a good thing.

They are unique individuals.

They are confusing, and confused.

They are often stronger than we are.

They can teach us as much as we've taught them.

They are inspiring, and still able to be inspired by us.

They are influential, and easily influenced.

They change every day.

They are DIFFERENT to us.

And they are the future.

Letting Go

When the first one leaves home, it's brutal.

It's like being unable to breathe, but hyperventilating at the same time.

It's like free-falling, but being crushed under a lorry.

It's like being a sad little dog wandering around helplessly looking for its favourite ball that it knows it hid somewhere special, but can't smell it any more.

But like all pains, all changes, all heartaches… it eases.

You get used to the missing, the longing, the wondering how they are.

You stop texting every twenty minutes.

You stop checking their Instagram feed to see if there's a story showing where they are, what they look like, who they're hanging out with.

You stop worrying when they don't call back.

You stop feeling a hole where they used to be.

It becomes the norm.

It really does.

And it's fine.

It's just the next stage – and it's actually quite nice because you can start to do more things you want to do.

And then you'll worry that you don't miss them enough, and don't care enough, and you're a shit mum because WHY DON'T YOU CALL THEM ALL THE TIME ANY MORE?

Stop. You're a human and you exist separately to your kids and that's a good, healthy thing.

It's hard.

It hurts.

It takes practice.

It takes time. Years. A lifetime, maybe.

And we never really do.

Sometimes we think we've 'let go', but we're actually clinging on like a bad simile to a page.

Why would we let go? They are our BABIES. We want to keep them close forever. Even when their coats are too huge to fit in the hallway.

But we have to do it. Take that leap, drop the lead, and let them go.

They'll run.

They'll fly.

They'll fall.

They'll get up again.

If they don't, you are always there to help.

But we have to let them go.

It's the best thing we'll ever do.

For ourselves, to become people again, separate from our offspring.

And for THEM.

PART 2
The Bit About YOU

Lost in Transition

Life goes in stages. Chapters. Blocks.

And so do we.

In each new stage we take on a new, different version of ourselves.

We are almost a different person.

Each one takes a bit of adjusting to and getting used to, and it's the transitions between two versions of us that are the hardest.

We have to try and figure out who we are now, in this new stage.

What we feel.

What we think.

What goals we have.

What we think we want.

What we actually want.

What we believe.

What we are prepared to believe.

Who we want to be.

Who we are.

From toddler to child. Child to teenager. Teenager to independent young adult.

Woman to mother.

And from mother of young children, to mother of independent young adults, moving away.

Some people thrive on change, uncertainty, adventure, unknowns.

But for most of us, some kind of certainty – and most of all certainty of SELF, of who we ARE – is essential. It's the *transitions* that destabilise and rock us.

We're suddenly cut loose, floating about in a sea of unknowns and new confusions; new opportunities and new worries; new dreams and new realities; new feelings and new fears; new excitements and new… 'WHO THE HELL AM I?'s.

We flail about, trying to find dry land, knowing we should be loving all this adventure and 'just enjoying the journey!' – but really, we just want to arrive in a huge comfy bed with complimentary biscuits and a lifetime's supply of expensive moisturiser.

We all land somewhere. It might not be the place we ever thought it would be, but it's somewhere.

It's the getting there that's the tricky bit.

Where Have I Gone?

You remember that bit back in Part 1 about how we used to bitch and moan about our kids not going to sleep when they were babies and toddlers, and how suddenly they start staying up later than we do when they hit the Middle Years, start taking showers at 9 p.m., doing homework until 10 p.m. and then group-chat all their mates until we shout at them to put the phone AWAY??

And that Limbo thing, where, despite being all but ignored at home, we still can't really go OUT on a whim because they're still too young to be left alone at home, and we need to be... y'know... responsible for them?

Well, in terms of MYSELF – as an individual, not a mum – this loss of any me-time at home was a huge shift in my life.

There seemed to be no peace, no time to think or be or do my own thing, until so late in the evening I was too tired to do it any more.

And, amazingly enough, very few of my friends were up

for popping out for a glass of wine at 10.30 p.m. either, after a full day of work and housework and parenting work.

It was like this when they were babies, obviously. We had to get babysitters if we wanted to do ANYTHING without the kids.

But I expected it then.

Now, all grown up in my Middle Years of parenting, I thought I'd leap joyfully back into Old Me, have my lovely evenings back to read, write, cook, go to a dance class, watch films I'd saved up for a decade, and find out who I was now.

But no. I just watched a bit of *MasterChef*, had a bath and went to sleep.

And it kind of got me down, if I'm honest. Because I just didn't expect this would happen.

I expected to have lots of newly available time to reconnect with myself. To have lots of me-time, at LAST, after years of THEM-time.

Instead, I became more disconnected from myself than ever, more distanced from a lot of things that had made me who I am, and from new feelings and thoughts about who I was NOW.

Who I had become, during the long, busy incubation period of Having Children.

I couldn't really spend any time with this new, Middle Years me, ask her what she wanted, what she liked, what she felt or thought about lots of things... because there was no TIME to do it.

So she got ignored.

When I finally did stop and meet her… I wasn't all that sure I knew who she was.

Or understood her.

Or even liked certain aspects of her very much.

I'm still trying to figure her out now, come to think about it.

It's a life's work, knowing who we are. But it does rather help if we can have the time – or make the time – to do it.

I Know Nothing

When my children were young, I felt staggeringly clever.

Any time one of them asked me a question I was right in there with the answer.

'Mummy, what's a trumpet?'

Bzzzzzzzz! I KNOW THIS ONE!

Every day felt like winning *Mastermind*.

And then somewhere, tucked quietly between an otherwise insignificant Wednesday afternoon and a chaotic Thursday morning, in a silent, unannounced leap, we leapt from:

'Mummy, what sound does a duck make?'

To:

'Mum, why did Trotsky stop being a supporter of the Menshevik Internationalists faction of the Russian Social Democratic Labour Party?'

The… what the fuck?

I had officially entered the stage of Not Knowing Anything.

My *Mastermind* days were over.

This sudden shift from smug genius to epic fuckwit came as a bit of a shock to my brain, and wasn't entirely helpful to my wobbly midlife self-esteem either.

HOW, when I'd gone to school and got a degree and once got TWO ANSWERS RIGHT on *University Challenge*, had I got to the age of forty knowing so unbelievably little??

I don't know who Nietzsche was, or what any tiny pieces of his philosophy were.

I don't know how the Second World War started. Or the First World War. Or the Balkans. (Why are they called the Balkans, anyway?)

I know the basics about Hitler shooting himself. (Or was it cyanide?) But I don't really know why or how it all happened.

I don't even know the chemical formula of flippin' cyanide.

I don't know how batteries work.

I don't know what macroeconomics is, or what it does. Is it a good thing? Do we like macroeconomics?

I don't know when Michelangelo lived or what he did, other than lie on a raised platform in the Sistine Chapel smoking cigars and wondering why his elbow hurt so much and why had nobody invented ibuprofen yet.

I didn't even know how to spell Michelangelo until I just googled it.

I don't even know if it's Spellcheck, or SpellcheckER.

I don't know how birds mate. Do they have a penis? Have you ever SEEN ONE? Do they dangle underneath?

Would bird-cum be useful in face-packs?

I haven't read *The Great Gatsby*. Or *The Great Escape*. Or *Great Expectations*.

I don't know what Watergate was all about, or exactly who the lady was who posed naked on that chair, or how the two are even related.

Was it Katherine Keener, or am I confusing her with an actress in the film *Capote*?

I don't know who the director of *Capote* was.

I'm not sure how Truman Capote links to Andy Warhol, but I have a feeling he does.

I'm not sure if Andy Warhol was British or American, or why he designed the cover of the Velvet Underground's album with the banana on it.

I don't really know what or when the Bauhaus movement was, even though I love Bauhaus architecture.

I can't tell you who the president of Romania is, or if they even have a president. Or where, within 1,000 miles, Romania IS, exactly.

I can't remember why, if you drop a cannonball and a ping-pong ball at the same time from the same height, they both hit the ground at the same time. If indeed they do. (Do they? Anyone got a cannonball, so we can try?)

I don't know how a car engine works, or a motor, or a dynamo.

I'm not sure what exactly Chairman Mao was the chairman of, or what that Red Book of his was. Was it by Jamie Oliver?

I literally. Know. Fuck. All.

And now, cruising their way through the National Curriculum of Facts, my kids were about to know more than me.

And I was about to feel monumentally stupid for the next ten years.

But you know what? Despite the extraordinary, gaping hole in my knowledge and education, I've somehow staggered through forty-five years of life reasonably successfully, produced three children, kept them alive and well for over twenty years, not got scurvy or syphilis, paid most of my bills, got a job, worked out whether plastic lids get recycled or not, administered a suppository into a crying toddler, filled in my online Self-Assessment Tax Return and once poured a cappuccino that looked pretty.

So I reckon I've done OK.

The upside of these Middle Years of feeling stupid is that our kids can finally prove useful, by teaching US a load of things we somehow never learned, or have forgotten.

And it's quite nice to use the old brain again, and sweat over some geometry of a Friday night.

Nobody Else Knows Anything Either

I had a sudden wobble in my Middle Years that I'd managed to get this far through my parenting life by sheer luck, blind optimism and by perfecting the art of bumbling along and bullshittry.

I became convinced that everyone else was doing things 'properly', had read the books and been to all the school meetings I'd missed, and was being a thorough, responsible, Good Parent, while I was about to be outed as a successful bumbler, bullshitter and fraud.

And then one happy day I realised that everyone else is bullshitting and bumbling along too. Nobody knows what they are doing, especially in the Middle Years of parenting.

The ones who appear to know lots of stuff just talk louder, and more confidently. That just makes them loud, confident frauds.

But frauds we all are, keeping calm(ish) and carrying on bumbling our way through.

Maybe that's exactly what parenting is.

Tired, Tired, Tired

I wrote a chapter in my first book called 'Tired, tired, tired'.

It was about the debilitating exhaustion that hits us in the first few months of pregnancy.

A decade later, I wrote a chapter in a book I was working on at the time called 'Tired, Tired, Tired', because I still was.

Today, four years after that, I am writing this little section, which appears to be called 'TIRED, TIRED, TIRED'.

I see a theme here.

The exhaustion of the Middle Years came as a surprise to me.

It felt like suddenly slamming back into the newborn/ breastfeeding/up-all-night times when I wandered around in a permanent state of Dehydrated Zombie.

After a blissful few years of almost existing normally on a nice seven or eight hours a night when my kids were somewhere between five and ten, I was now back to requiring so much sleep I made hibernating dormice look hyperactive.

If anyone in my house needs to speak to me after 7 p.m.,

they know they'll find me crawling towards the bathroom, moaning desperately about being SO TIRED I'M ABOUT TO DIE. YOU HAVE NO IDEA WHAT IT'S LIKE TO BE THIS TIRED!! LEAVE ME! SAVE YOURSELVES!

No amount of sleep is enough for me.

Just to make things even better, the Middle Years are also when many of us develop insomnia.

Me at 9 a.m. – literally hurts to stay awake.

Me at 11 p.m. – WHO WANTS TO PARTY?

I'd do anything to be able to stock-pile sleep and get regular fixes throughout the day. I'd put some in freezer bags, and in my glasses case, and in my handbag and down my tights.

The thing I hate most about being this tired is not just the ghastly feeling of tiredness itself, or that it makes me grouchy and miserable, look ancient and feel horrendous.

What I hate most about it is that I have to sacrifice such a HUGE proportion of my already pitifully small quantities of free time just to try and be SODDING WELL ASLEEP. I can't remember the last time I stayed up to watch a WHOLE FILM, without sitting there in such pain from tiredness, and wracked by nervous tension about how shit I'm going to feel the next day if I don't go to bed right NOW, and anxiety that when I try to fall asleep I'll be hit with über-awakeness until 3 a.m. and feel even WORSE, that I couldn't follow the storyline beyond the opening credits.

My ex, by contrast, could sit there watching *Family Guy*

until 2 a.m., then come to bed, fall asleep, wake up five hours later and go to work. Just like that.

Bastard.

It's not fair to hate someone for being able to stay awake.

But I did. I hated him for his ability to stay awake more than I will ever tell him.

What infuriates me about this life-sapping tiredness, is that it seems utterly inexplicable. I don't DO anything any more that requires me to need so much sleep!

I'm not growing a child in my abdomen. I'm not feeding a baby all night. I'm not working night shifts or going clubbing every night. Or even ONE night.

I'm just... living. Normally.

But that's it.

In the Middle Years, most of us are TIRED.

Not moment to moment, but accumulative tired.

Piled-up, built-up, stocked-up TIRED.

By this stage we've done at least a decade of heavy-duty family-ing.

House moves, renovations, travel, job stresses, the loss of relatives, marriage problems or breakdown, arguments, children, school issues, in-law clashes, break-ins, illnesses, pets and never-ending laundry. We may also have had major health issues that have left us tired, or are here now and exhaust us. Or our partners or other family members might have health issues that make us tired.

It's like a giant vat of Lifetired, that seeps in from all sides.

So yes. We are generally pretty TIRED, TIRED, TIRED.

If you think you're the only one crawling to bed two hours before you want to, and before everyone on The Socials appears to be going to bed, rest assured that you're not.

We're all in there, dropping off before the ten o'clock bongs.

And if that's what it takes to survive the next few years, then that's what we gotta do.

Just occasionally it's a good plan to say: 'OH SOD YOU, SLEEP!' and stay out until 3 a.m. You will feel unspeakably terrible for a week, and age five years for every minute after midnight you stay out. But you will at least have had some goddam FUN. And fun is important.

Orgasms Are Your Friend

It doesn't matter if you don't feel like it, you have no time, you're kinda stressed or just your life is generally non-orgasmic in every imaginable way... go have one, on your own and just for YOU.

Do whatever it takes.

Have a bath. Let your kids watch all the crap on telly you never let them watch so 'Mum can have a little lie-down because she's got a headache.'

Watch porn. Read the news. Whatever floats your fun-boat.

Go come. Orgasms work.

The New (Real) Forty

I remember my mother's fortieth birthday vividly.

I remember everything about the evening: what we had to eat, what I wore, what we talked about, even the colour of the light in the dining room. But most of all I remember thinking, 'When I am forty I am NEVER going to be like this.'

I vowed there and then that when I smashed the big Four Oh I'd house a house full of sexy, exciting people wearing sexy, exciting clothes, we'd all be swearing freely at the dinner table, laughing heartily at pointless, silly things we'd seen that day that had absolutely no academic or intellectual merit whatsoever, and my kids would all be allowed to wear make-up if they wanted to.

Every day. On both eyes.

My fortieth was going to be BLINDING.

The reality went a bit like this:

October 2013

6.45 p.m.

The kitchen.

It's my fortieth birthday.

We were going to go out but I'm feeling too knackered, and I have a massive spot growing above my left eyebrow.

Also, I have to finish writing a riveting article about kids' party bags by tomorrow, and one of my kids needs collecting from a school trip to Somewhere at 9 p.m. because there was traffic on the M6 and two of the children in Class 4A were sick.

We're also not feeling very financially flush right now, thanks to all of our offspring requiring new trainers AND jeans at the same time.

So I have a bath, watch the first twenty minutes of Atonement*, again, and fall asleep. Happy birthday, crazy, sexy, exciting me.*

Social Life 1: Not Going Out

I had a dream, last night.

This is where all similarities between myself and Martin Luther King end. It's also a very dubious similarity, as my dream actually happened not last night but years ago, when I was scraping dried peas off the bottom of my son's high chair, and Martin's dream was, arguably, a tad more historically important than mine.

Anyway. My little dream, such as it was.

I dreamed, based, now I think about it, on no evidence whatsoever but just a desperate NEED to believe it in order to survive the next few years of toddler-dom, that as my children got older I would reclaim that thing I lost ten years ago somewhere down the back of the nappy bin:

MY SOCIAL LIFE.

Surely, when it no longer took calling in the UN Peacekeeping envoy just to leave the house for half an hour, I would be able to just walk out of the door, on a whim, any time, and GO OUT.

***

What actually happens when you want to go out in the Middle Years is this:

Step 1. Become breathless with a sudden, overwhelming urge not to be in the house any more, so as to a) avoid proximity to the fridge/dishwasher/husband/laptop/ laundry/ work deadlines/teenage angst and the sight of the landslide that is your own face in the bathroom mirror, and b) be closer to nice people who understand how maddening a) is.

Step 2. Send emergency text to eight friends and five people you don't really know all that well but would be prepared to share booze with if you had to, asking if they would like to go out for a drink. Any time, but preferably now. RIGHT NOW.

Step 3. Receive two replies containing variations of:

'Oh would LOVE to, but I can't! Child X has been throwing up all week, and work is a nightmare right now, and I am SO exhausted! Shall we try for next week?? Sorry!! Xxx'

Assume the others were too tired to reply at all.

Step 4. Do not go out.

Step 5. Feel old and boring, made worse by a painful awareness that you're actually quite glad you didn't go out, because now you'll feel fresh in the morning, and anyway you wanted to watch series two of *The Crown*, even though you've already seen it three times.

I can go for months having this kind of arrangement ping-pong with friends. At least 50 per cent of my texts are of this nature.

My record was a year.

At that point I just went to the pub by myself and was carried home two hours later by a local carpenter.

The tragic fact is that at any given time at this stage of life, it's a dead-cert bet that at least two of your four closest friends will have one or more children who are vomiting, doing exam revision, experiencing soul-crushing wardrobe dilemmas, a sudden attack of acne, Facebook bullying or love-related problems that cause total emotional breakdown, tendencies towards self-harm with paper clips and severe door-slamming.

The remaining two have work to catch up on, an unspecified medical condition that prevents them from drinking, a Relate meeting, or are off to the gym in case the Relate thing doesn't work out and they need semi-presentable buttocks to attract a rebound mate.

We know this is the case, but it's hard to believe other people aren't out having a fabulous time when we are in having a reasonably unacceptable time.

It's part of the human condition of self-loathing and social paranoia that if we don't see our friends for more than a week we automatically assume they are all out snorting wild things and drinking wild things and generally living it up like the wild, crayzee, mortgage-paying parents of teenage children they are.

This assumption is not helped by social mediaaaaaaa showing everyone apparently having a wildish time, behind a wrinkle-reducing filter.

But they are mostly not having a wildish time.

They are at home, just like you and me, channel-hopping, folding school uniforms and wondering if the kitchen wall needs a repaint.

So, enjoy it. Stay in! Eat ice cream straight out of the tub with your fingers. Do a face-pack in the bath. Drink herbal tea out of your favourite mug.

Nobody will think any worse of you, because they're probably doing the same.

This is one of the giant plus points about the Middle Years: we have nothing to prove to anyone, and we don't have to give the slightest shit about what other people think of us.

You stay in, if you want to.

You're in strong company.

Then tweet about what a mad time you're having in a wine bar.

Social Life 2: Going Out

THAT SAID… from time to time the stars all align: Venus goes retrograde and grows sideburns, and Saturn does something special with Uranus, usually only reserved for birthdays, and…

YOU. GO. OUT.

Going out in the Middle Years goes like this:

Send five emoticon-splattered texts asking to move the meeting time back by half an hour each time, because you are 'shiiiiiit, running late!!'

Spend an hour trying to find something to wear that is neither too old nor too young, or both.

Be told by teenage daughter that if you go out like that she will ACTUALLY DIE.

Change.

Change back again.

Hate self, but decide it'll have to do.

Leave house.

Go back for phone, keys, emergency chocolate bar, concealer. Lip balm. More concealer.

Walk into pub.

Look around. Feel older than most of the exhibits in the British Museum.

See friends.

Feel better.

Promise not to talk about children or work.

Drink one glass of wine.

Get pissed.

Drink another, because YOU ARE OUT, so you must. This might be the last time you are out drinking before Prince George loses his virginity.

Feel spinny. Slur.

Talk about children. And work. And men.

Cry.

Fall asleep into a packet of crisps at 10 p.m.

Have a hangover for a week.

And THAT, my friend, is a bloody good night out for 90 per cent of people over the age of thirty-five.

***

NOTE:

After years of careful and dedicated research I can reveal that, in midlife, the formula for how long it takes a hangover to go away, is this:

T = x (v+g+4w) -5s + c^9

Where:

T is time in hours

x is your age

v is vodka

g is gin

w is cheap wine

s is number of hours of sleep you got the night before

c is the number of your children who woke you up during the night to tell you that their ballet leotard needs to be washed BY TOMORROW, and by the way, Mum, I have a VERY IMPORTANT maths assignment which counts for half of my marks this year and will go on my university application form, and I need a new calculator for it. Now.

Accordingly, if you go out on a Saturday night you should be starting to feel a little better some time towards the end of the following week.

So long as you schedule this into your diary, and block out all important meetings such as speaking to your spouse or children and dealing with any Big Schooling Decisions until the little men have stopped using a pneumatic drill in your cranium, all will be well and you CAN go out for two and a half glasses of wine.

You midlife rebel, you.

Where Are My Friends?

When our kids go up to secondary school, and often a little before, most of us stop doing the school run.

This is largely because we can't really be arsed any more, and anyway they usually bugger off to a friend's house the minute we turn up, rendering the entire trip pointless, except for us to act as a pack horse for all their clobber. But mainly the school run gets the chop because our kids would die of shame if anything as mortifying as BEING SEEN NEAR THEIR PARENT occurred.

I also reckoned by that stage, that if my kids couldn't manage to get from my house to school without a chaperone and a personal bag carrier, I should probably take them to my local recycling centre and leave them there.

The end of the school run heralded a huge change in my parenting life. And not in the ways I had expected.

Stupidly, I had never really thought about the negative sides.

I was SO desperate never to do the mind-numbing trudge

to school every morning in the rain carrying book bags and PE kits, fancy dress costumes and violins, I'd have sold a kidney for the chance to give it up.

For about a month after it all petered out, it was fantastic.

Every morning after my kids left for school I'd stay at home, dancing in the kitchen in my pants, shouting, 'FREEEEDOOOOOMMMMMMM!!!!! YOU'RE AT SCHOOL! I'M IN MY PANTS AT HOME!! DANCIIIIIING! AHAHAAAAAA!!!'

But then, it happened. I got cold in my pants, and there was nobody to share the moment with. It was just me and… solitude.

Silence.

No mates.

Just knickers.

The people I'd spent the last decade seeing on a daily basis, having a natter and a laugh with, a bitch and a gossip with, being told all the things I didn't know about because my son had left the letter at the bottom of his school bag covered in mud, people I had human INTERACTION with… had disappeared.

I stopped seeing people, because there was no forced occasion to.

From this point on, seeing other parents became an effort. A job. Something I had to add to the 'to-do' list.

Endless texts were exchanged, mutually suitable dates were never found, because everyone was busy being busy/ill/

exhausted/watching *Bake Off*. Emails pinged back and forth, all of us trying to keep in touch, organise dinners or drinks. And always falling foul of 'I'd love to, but…' (See 'Not Going Out'.)

With our children now kindly taking themselves to school, our working days suddenly got three hours longer, and most of us ran back to something approaching that hallowed joy of paid, full-time work.

And because we worked more, what nanoseconds of 'free time' we had were no longer spent chatting in the playground about next week's trip to the museum or debating the success or otherwise of Mrs P's breast implants, but catching up on housework, emails, laundry and shopping.

Communication with my mum friends became zilch on a daily or even weekly basis, almost overnight. Sure, we'd bump into each other in the Co-op, in town, at various school events, and do that little game of 'Hi! Haven't seen you for AGES! God, we MUST go out soon. Yes?? Let's do diaries…'

And we mean it. We all yearn for that contact, and those friendships.

But then we get home and it's all forgotten in a sea of family/work-life-ing.

I'm painting a bleak picture here. It's not THAT bad.

But the core group that existed so strongly for so long really takes a battering in the Middle Years, where work-life takes over children-life, we move on to other things, and we part ways with people who were once an integral part of our every day – whether they were great friends or not, at least they were THERE.

It made me sad, at times.

Isolated. Kinda lonely. And I didn't expect it.

I know that a lot of this isolation was because I'm self-employed, and work from home.

If you work in an office or with other people, the loneliness is generally not so bad. You might make new friends there, and chat with colleagues every day. But if you don't, or if like millions of parents you've carved out a career for yourself to work around your childcare needs, you're pretty much alone for most of the day, and it can become staggeringly solitary and even a bit depressing.

Keeping up with even one or two friends from the Early Years is really worth the investment in time. You might not feel you need it right now, but there's more shit to hit the fan in the Middle Years than at any other time, and it's the friends who shared the puke-laden, tantrum-heavy Early Years with us who are the ones we really need now.

Pick up the phone.

Call. MAKE A DATE in your diaries.

Go on the bloody school run if you have to! Just stay connected.

Little Friend Fact

We only really need one or two friends.

Good friends. Solid friends. The Golden 'you can call me at 3 a.m. and I'll be there for you' Top-Rung friends.

That's honestly enough.

Everyone else is like... second-rung.

Lovely 'n' all, but you don't need twenty-five friends. In fact, you can't HAVE twenty-five friends when you're over thirty-five and have children. It takes far too much time, energy and giving a fuck, and most of us are too knackered and busy.

Online friends are awesome too – and yes, THEY CAN BE ACTUAL FRIENDS, even though you've never met them in 'real life'. I've made closer, more honest, supportive, kind, generous, wonderful, life-saving friends online than anywhere else, and they've become a vital part of my 'real', offline life.

Those people who seem to have reams and reams of awesome friends? Let 'em. If that's what they need – or even have, truly – then good for them. That's their life.

If you are OK with one or two, and they are Top-Rung friends, you're good to go, and will swim safely through the Middle Years without armbands.

Hello, Stranger

Strangers can be the best friends you'll never have.

I love befriending strangers.

I'm the textbook Embarrassing Mum who starts actual conversations with the waiter or randoms on a bus, with slightly too loud laughs, and my kids want to die.

But I find strangers the easiest of all to talk to, and just... have a moment with.

These are my 'moment-friends'. My little brushes with humanity and kindness that have seen me through wobbles and sadnesses I'd otherwise have crumbled under. And for me, they are worth as much as any long-term friendship anyone could have.

I've found huge solace, support, humanity, relief, laughs, genuine emotional and true connection, and moments that I think quite honestly have saved my life, with strangers on a train, on a bus, in a café, just passing in the street, in the queue at Zara, at an airport check-in desk and online.

There are good people out there. Sometimes all it takes is a 'hello'.

One little chat over the price of an apple in the market, one shared moment, look, smile, sigh, eye-roll, whatever it is.

It's a SHARED moment.

And those are what keep me going.

Talk to that waiter.

He or she might be the friend you need right now.

Social Media Rules (No It Doesn't)

For anyone born before about 1985, social media is still a 'new thing'.

We weren't brought up with it.

We didn't grow with it as a natural extension of our fingertips.

No previous generation in the Middle Years of family life has ever had to share their stage with social media.

And this is both good, and bad.

I love social media.

And I hate it.

I love the beautiful, amazing things it shows me that I'd otherwise never see.

I love the people it brings into my life that I'd otherwise never meet.

I love the conversations I have on there, the window into other worlds, other lives and other places.

I love how much it can help my work, inspire my creativity, boost me when I'm flagging.

I love how it opens new doors to opportunities I'd never otherwise have.

I love the truth it shows me.

I love the company, and the connections.

But…

I hate how it saps my time.

I hate how it's in the room, when I should be in the room with the person I'm in the room with.

I hate how it can kill my self-confidence.

I hate how it can zap my creative flow.

I hate how many flipping doors it shows me, that I now feel I need to open, immediately, or I'll miss out on the BEST OPPORTUNITY OF MY LIFE.

I hate how it lies to me.

And I hate that I still fall foul of that, like some dickhead who's forgotten about FILTERS!

I hate how it shuts me off from the company all around me in my real life.

I hate how it disconnects me.

I just need to remember to tame the beast, occasionally, and PUT IT AWAY.

A few helpful things I've learned along the way, from myself and others:

Our social media is exactly that: OUR social media. Our playground, in the way we want it to be. For us. Nobody else. That's the exact beauty of it. And we forget that, SO OFTEN!

We owe social media nothing. We don't need to please it, feed it or care about it. We can put it down any time we like, and pick it up again when we fancy a cuddle.

It's the IDEAL pet. And it doesn't shed hair.

If people out there don't like what we post, say, write, do, wear, don't do, that's their problem not ours. If you lose Instagram followers, it's OK. It doesn't mean loads of people don't like you. It just means you have fewer Instagram followers.

You can walk away from it. It's OK. Really. It will still be there when you get back.

You don't lose 800 followers if you go away for the weekend and stop showing them photos of your lunch.

But, my work will suffer!

No, it won't.

This 'work' is actually POTENTIAL WORK, as yet undefined by any science or, actually, bankable results.

You will not become irrelevant and stop influencing things. You probably don't anyway. The things you DO influence are the ones you actually spend time with when you're not spending time trying so hard to influence things.

IF YOU DETOX FOR A WHILE NOTHING WILL HAPPEN.

Two people might message you to check you're OK. They are the good ones. The kind ones. The actual HUMAN ones.

The rest are follow fodder. They're there mainly for their

OWN gain, not yours. Your likes? That's about algorithms. They mean, literally, NOTHING. And without them, you are still you.

Uninstall if you have to. Lock your phone in a safe if you have to.

Just GET AWAY FROM IT.

You'll feel better for it. And, most probably, so will everyone who cares about you.

Body Stuff

One of the most difficult things about living in a house with teenagers is the sudden, blindingly stark contrast between their radiant, sexually awakening beauty and youth, and… ourselves.

This is not helped by the fact that they spend most of the weekends slouching about in a Lolita-esque way, in nothing but Topshop pants barely covered by a T-shirt, helpfully accentuating the fact that a) their bum still looks like a bum, not a cauliflower b) their breasts have yet to be introduced to gravity and c) they have skin, not cow hide.

Just remember, they are young. And we are not as young. Go and look at photos of sun-weathered octogenarians and feel better about yourself.

HAIR

Something weird happens to hair in midlife: it suddenly decides it's time to feng shui itself, and REARRANGE.

Without warning or permission, hair starts moving itself from one part of our body to another; notably from our head to... all other parts.

Legs, pubes, inner thigh, upper lip, nose, toes, you name it.

Just NOT head.

This is all kinds of bad. Hair should never be allowed to rearrange itself – this is *our* job, even if forty years and six sets of curling tongs haven't taught us how to do it properly, or without setting fire to our hands, most of our hair and the bedroom rug.

Midlife hair also cruelly does what the rest of our body has struggled to do for three decades: it thins.

Rapidly.

Total bastard, bastard, BASTARD hair.

These days what's on my head is not so much 'hair' as occasional patches of un-baldness.

It's got so bad recently that I've had to adopt a comb-over across the back of my head to stop drivers behind me from being blinded by my scalp-shine from their headlights.

Honestly though, one day it was there, dutifully hanging out of my head, and then suddenly... it was on my bathroom floor. It was in my hairbrush. It was on my clothes, all over the sofa, in the laundry basket, and occasionally popping up in someone's pasta.

But not on my head.

When it's wet, the whole lot together is now thinner than a single strand of quick-cook spaghetti.

Happily, I discovered three things I could do to feel less terrible about my hair.

Cut it. Almost nobody looks worse with shorter hair. Fact.

Never look at Young People's hair. I can't advise this strongly enough. You could stuff a king-sized duvet with what grows out of one teenager's head and still have enough left over to weave blankets for an entire Mongolian village. It's monstrously unfair.

Know the style that suits you now. Not when you were fifteen. Or eight. Or twenty-five. NOW. Adopt it and wear it like the Midlife Winner you are.

We interrupt this page to bring you Very Important Information

In the Middle Years it's no longer enough just to look at your face in the mirror, straight on.

No. You now need mirrors and lights on all sides, *including underneath.*

Terrifying things lurk, fester and grow in places you've never looked at before, but must now monitor with Eagle Eyes, and possibly a helicopter search light.

One such place is just under your chin.

For there, sprouting like an antenna sending distress signals to the mother witch-beacon, you will find your first chin hair.

Thick. Black. Devastating.

When you've stopped screaming and ordering broomsticks on Amazon, do this:

Get tweezers; pull it out; do not look at it; throw it away; never tell anyone about it.

EVER.

And now let us never speak of this again.

LEGS

Ohhhhhhh how I wish I'd enjoyed my legs more when I was in my twenties.

At the time I thought they were either a) too fat or b) too pregnant or c) too veiny or d) too post-baby-weight-loss skinny.

I now realise, with the handy Binoculars of Hindsight, that back then my legs were actually fit and firm and gorgeous and fan-fucking-tastic… even though they looked a bit wonky in a miniskirt because they are wiry runner's legs and go inwards a bit at the knees, like a stick-man doing the Charleston.

Here are a few facts about my Middle Years legs:

I now have legs that sometimes look as if they have another pair of legs inside them. If you press down on the skin of either of my legs pretty much anywhere, you can see an entire other lumpy person under there, hiding. It's quite disconcerting. I wonder what they DO in there all day. Maybe they could, like, come out and help with all the laundry?

It is still impossible for me to shave the bony bits around my ankles without severing an artery, even after twenty-five years of practice. So they're covered in unsightly scars where I've basically shaved all my skin off in a rush to get to a meeting without tripping over my leg hairs on my way.

VEINS

A few summers ago, we got lost driving through south-west France. As luck would have it my son noticed that the spider veins on the back of my left leg formed an almost exact road map of the Languedoc region, complete with service stations. Thus it was that we made it on time for our Shuttle crossing. If I ever feel bad about my veiny Midlife Legs, I try to remember this, and feel better. I also try whenever possible to remember not to stand next to either of my daughters when they are wearing micro-skirts.

While we're at it… varicose veins. OMGGGG.

They just… arrive. And won't leave. Since turning forty I've worn tights with the same denier as my age, to hide them. I look forward to my sixties when I'll basically be wearing tarpaulin on my legs.

KNEES

I used to have knees.

When my children were babies, I used them to crawl across the living room floor, collecting small pieces of Lego in my kneecap along the way.

As I got older and my cartilage decided to retire to Bali, my knees became a hot topic of conversation between me and a physio in my gym.

But somewhere around the age of forty and twenty minutes, something awful happened to my knees, thrusting them centre stage in my list of Life's Great Worries, and forcing me to ask HOW I HAD NEVER NOTICED THIS BEFORE.

While waiting for a train, I noticed a small piece of toilet paper that seemed to have got stuck to the bottom of my shoe. Casually glancing downwards to see whether I could remove it without exposing my pants to everyone at platform 8, my eyes came to a screaming halt halfway down my leg, to where a perfectly ordinary, uninteresting knee had once resided, and…

WHAT IS THAT??

There. Just above the knee cap.

An OVERHANG.

Rumpling and folding, concertina-like above my knee like those thick, brown tights that grannies wear, piling up near their grankles.

Only it wasn't tights: it was SKIN.

This, my friends, was Knee Overhang.

No matter how much you go to the gym or drink collagen milkshakes, there is nothing you can do about Knee Overhang.

In a further twist of cruel biology, tensing your muscles to 'pull' the skin back upwards makes it worse.

This is madness, because the Universally Acknowledged Rule of Loose Flesh is that if you tense it, it looks better. Everyone knows that. But knees have their own sub-clause, which exempts them from all tensing-rule-compliance after the age of thirty-five.

Nothing will remove Knee Overhang except surgery, and I'd rather spend the two grand on loads of nice notepads and a shower that doesn't dribble.

So, I'll just live with it, and use it as a handy place to store a receipt if I've got no pockets.

Given that my legs probably aren't going to get a whole lot better between now and my nineties, and I'll look back on my forties when I'm in my sixties and wish I'd enjoyed them more back then, or rather now (keep up please...), I reckon I might as well just get 'em out and enjoy what's there.

Oh, and if you're travelling anywhere near Carcassonne by car, give me a shout and I'll check my left thigh for directions.

SKIN

The droop.

Here's a fun thing to do if you're over thirty-five and want to feel fantastic about yourself: find a mirror and hang your head upside down in front of it.

You'll notice almost immediately that you can't see anything.

This is because the hold-all bags of under-eye skin that you've valiantly tried to prop up with Polyfilla and concealer have now broken free of their beige camouflage and slopped their way up over your eyeballs in a dermatological landslide. Your cheeks, meanwhile, now pulled 'up' towards your hair by gravity, are just shoving the whole saggy, loathsome lot even further towards your forehead.

If you're doing it properly you should now be squinting at a face that resembles an elephant's ball-sack being squeezed into a jelly mould three sizes too small.

Aaaand we're done.

You may now stand up, wait for the blood to gush out of your brain and then reach for the nearest antidepressant.

I hadn't noticed how bad the Midlife Skin Slump was until I did the upside-down-face thing.

Obviously, I'd noticed some changes. LONG gone are the days when I can wake up, splash water on my face and leave the house with nothing more than a dollop of £2.99 tinted moisturiser.

Years of merciless, unprotected sunbathing back in the eighties and nineties – aargh! REGRET! – four pregnancies, decades of mothering, and several years of Marital Disquiet, Depression and Sadness have left my skin looking like a Jackson Pollock of marks, patches, blotches and craters.

NOTE: never ever ever ever ever ever buy a magnifying mirror.

You're welcome.

SPOTS

Oh, c'mon now. MIDLIFE ACNE?

I had fairly spot-prone skin as a teenager, but that kind of goes with The Territory so I just got on with it and developed staggeringly low self-esteem, like a good girl.

But now, deeply embedded in my forties when The Territory now includes receding gums and nipple-sag, spots should just bugger the hell off.

We have enough to be dealing with.

But no. STILL, THEY COME. I wake up some mornings to discover that, deep in my face's underground system, a mob of angry, repressed bacteria have decided to organise a rally and congregate under my jaw bone, arming themselves for a mass demonstration that takes a week to come to a head even if I DO bathe my entire face in TCP the second I feel a tingle.

When they finally come out and start spreading their grimness all over my face, they take three weeks to clear up.

I can't blame puberty. I can't blame a poor facial regime.

I can just accept that it happens – and get better concealer.

Face treats

Facials work. Period.

Treating your midlife skin like fucking Royalty once in a while does it the world of good. In fact, treating your whole body nicely once in a while, and getting someone to pummel and squeeze and knead and soothe it with things that smell of Other People's More Relaxing Lives, is a lifesaver.

Even if you can only manage one a year – which is about my average – it's worth it.

TEETH

Midlife teeth are a nightmare.

Mine were near-perfect until I hit forty, and then just sort of... fell the fuck apart.

From there it's been almost constant cavities, root canal treatments, tooth extractions, dry sockets, agony, painkillers, antibiotics and general tooth hell.

If, like me, the Middle Years have made you kinda stressy, it's likely you're a grinder – and not in a good, sexy-grinding way. I wore almost all of my enamel away while I was 'sleeping', apparently not entirely peacefully, and this caused all manner of problems I won't bore you with here, but shit gets real if you grind, OK?

A night-time tooth guard sorted it, but I wish I'd checked years earlier.

Go to the dentist. Get your teeth sorted. Save yourself a LOT of pain and money.

The Midlife Mind

When I had children, I expected my body to change. I'm THAT smart.

I also expected my mind to change for a while, and I was reasonably clued-up about postnatal depression and general baby-years meltdown.

But I thought it would be just that: postnatal. Or confined to the early, sleep-deprived years, at most.

I NEVER expected my mind to change the way it did in the Middle Years of parenting, almost a decade after I last squeezed a baby down my birth canal.

Instead of getting itself sorted and stable now that my kids were a little older, and I had a BREAK from them more, my brain decided to hand in its P45 and say:

'Right, that's it, I'm done. I've seen you through three rounds of childbirth, ten nativity plays, five unbroken years of nits, three bouts of chicken pox, two disastrous holidays to Cornwall, 1,856 potato prints, seventy-five emergency nappy changes in Tesco and a nasty case of oral thrush.

'I'm done. You go sort your shit out yourself, because frankly, my love, I need a holiday.'

And that was that.

Far from being a time when we are 'finally sorted' or have learned to understand ourselves properly, put our own teenage angsts and worries behind us and grown into strong and stable adults with a handle on it all, the Middle Years are actually a time when loads of us have our first huge mental health KABOOM.

The first panic attack.

The first major bout of depression.

The first breakdown.

The first signs of bipolar disorder.

The first prescription of antidepressants.

The first referral to a psychiatrist.

The first problems with alcohol.

Or food, or drugs or YOU NAME IT.

Rather than hitting a glorious stage of SORTEDNESS, now we've hit our awesome Middle Years and grown confidently into our new, more wrinkly but comfortable skin, for many of us a whole lot of mental health issues only start when our kids have grown up a little, and taken the slack off.

And maybe it's partly for exactly this reason.

It's like that thing where you're working on a gigantic piece of work that's kept you fully, exhaustingly occupied to the exclusion of all else for months and months, and you just keep going and going and going because you have to, and then the deadline arrives, you hand it all in and…

CRASH.

You get flu. And spots. And you feel horrendous. And cry ALL THE TIME, when you thought you'd be at your happiest for ages.

It's a bit like that, but where the body of work you've handed in is… your kids.

We're also just older now, and more worn by a LOT of stuff that's happened.

Our minds are also older and more worn, and that's when the problems can start.

I found the Middle Years to be a time of enormous mental challenge and change, new problems, disappointments, fears, traumas, shocks and knocks I didn't expect to face, and all in all a bit of a mind-fuck, if I'm honest.

It's not unusual; in fact, it's extremely common.

The good news is that we can be put back together again.

It might take a while, but it's possible.

There is therapy, medication if required, yoga, meditation, going for long walks, talking to friends and masturbation. So many things are available to us, to help us through the mental wobbles.

And perhaps the most helpful of all, at times, is just knowing that we're by NO means the only ones going through it.

YOU got this. WE got this. Together.

Grey-scale

The state of our mental health, much like our physical health, fluctuates.

Sometimes it's fine, and other times it's… a bit wrecked.

Throughout our lives, we slide up and down the mental health 'wellness scale' like a hula-hoop on a piece of string at a birthday party.

It doesn't mean we're weird, weak, best avoided or there's something wrong with us.

It probably just means we are normal humans, with normal human problems.

Why we expect anything different to this is totally bizarre to me.

Are we always *physically* well?

No.

Sometimes we get flu. Or back pain. Or piles. Or conjunctivitis.

And nobody freaks out.

Similarly, sometimes we get anxiety attacks. We suffer a bout of depression. We drink too much. We lose all our self-confidence. We have eating disorders. We get insomnia. We just… lose our mental shit for a while.

The Middle Years are no different. Most of us are not suddenly better able to deal with it, just because we're a bit older and supposedly wiser.

Arguably, we're worse able to deal with it, for the same reasons.

We're older, and wiser to the strangeness, difficulty and enormity of life. Of children growing up. Of illness, and sadness, disappointment and stress, trial and error, love and loss.

But at least now we have reached a stage of our lives where we know ourselves a little, know that it's expected, it's normal and it's OK.

The Post-post-post-post-baby Blues

I'm going to write some things about sadness, now.

So that's fun.

Sadness is an emotion we're not very good at dealing with in our culture, I think.

We try to hush it up the moment it starts, make a joke and laugh it off, make excuses for it, find reasons for it, or say how silly we are to feel sad, when, hey, we're still ALIVE, right?

Depression, we understand a bit. But sadness, we don't seem to 'get', or help in the way it needs.

It's so buried and silenced it's almost as if we're terrified of it, because we don't understand what it is, or why it comes, or what to DO about it, especially is there's no obviously accountable cause.

In the Middle Years there's a huge amount of sadness for many people, and I really don't think we acknowledge or deal with it very well.

When I give book talks about parenting in the Middle Years, or mental health and wellbeing generally, this is the subject that gets the most head-nods and the strongest emotional response; SADNESS is the part people usually want to come and talk to me about afterwards. I've even had people crying while I've been talking about it. (A fabulous confidence booster, that one.)

So here are some thoughts about sadness in the Middle Years, in case any of it applies to you, and helps you.

Crying

I'm not sure when I first noticed that I was feeling sad. I think it might have been when I realised I'd cried several times a day, every day, for nearly a year. That, I rationalised, was possibly not very healthy.

I think my children were about fourteen, twelve and nine at the time. Something like that. I can't pin-point it exactly.

Such is the nature of such things. They just sidle up and come in for a quick hello, and then, before you know it, they've moved in, taken your favourite seat in front of the telly, and have become your mood.

There was no 'event' or moment in particular to which I could attribute this sadness. It wasn't like a postnatal depression or shock. (If it was, it was SPECTACULARLY delayed!)

Basically, over a period of a year or so, I noticed that I felt… heavy.

Down. Lacking in happiness. Or lightness.

I was still able to feel happy, when I was out and about with friends, say, or chatting on social media, or walking through London looking at the sun on the Soho pavements. But even my feelings of happiness were tinged with a heaviness; like a sadness at feeling happy.

Sadness at how beautiful that pavement light was.

My baseline mood at home was more subdued than it had been for years, or possibly ever, and lacked my usual (probably annoying) brightness and *joie de vivre*. I felt as if I was just plodding along through my life, with increasing weariness.

And I cried. A LOT.

The crying would come without warning, and in the kind of floods that merit their own TV documentary.

It could start within minutes of waking up. And then again in the middle of the morning. At lunchtime. And at night.

I could still go out, talk to people, laugh, smile, drink coffee merrily, do my job well and be generally extremely jolly if needed to be; but the second I walked away, the face-tidal-wave would start again.

I had to start wearing mascara so waterproof it was basically a Sharpie pen.

I could even cry when I was out running, which is pretty bloody difficult because you can't breathe.

It felt as if my body was desperately trying to empty itself of that little-known UNESCO World Heritage Site, the Bottomless Lake of Melancholy.

At these times it felt impossible for me to imagine a time

when I wouldn't cry any more. There was no state of not crying, or not wanting to cry, available to me.

And I didn't understand WHY. Why was I crying??

The sun was out. I had a job that I enjoyed, I had good coffee and limitless access to pumpkin seeds. I had few but good friends, which is all one needs.

I had three copies of *The Royal Tenenbaums* on DVD, my kids didn't hate me enough to have run away from home yet and I could still use a trampoline without wetting myself – WHY was I crying??

I've talked with many people, women and men, in this stage of life – and I do mean STAGE, not age – and it does seem that Chronic Sadness can descend just at the point when we thought it was about to get easier.

It's maybe that Kids Growing Up thing.

That Loss of Joy thing.

That Limbo thing.

That Tired, Tired, Tired thing.

That Crossroads thing.

That What If thing.

That whole Middle Years thing.

It wasn't just me. It isn't just you (if indeed it's you at all).

But, sometimes, it might need a little help to shift it. A talk, some counselling, a new hobby, meeting new people, sharing what you're feeling.

Because trying to carry it all alone just doesn't work.

You are all the stronger for realising it, admitting it, and getting help sorting it.

Meet My New Friends, Anxiety and Panic

I had my first panic attack when I was thirty-five. I was driving along the A14 in a perfectly un-anxious way, listening to the radio, all good, when, without any warning, fanfare or announcement on my brain's PA system, I had a panic attack.

Palms sweating, pulse racing, panting, wide-eyed yet blinded in terror, I thought I was going to faint.

This was accompanied by a strange sensation that the world was too enormously, unmanageably BIG, and sunlight was too bright, and the sky was too empty and sky-ish, and the concept of Time was too strange and my children were too unable to live if anything happened to me, and everything went white and sparkly before I hurtled onto the hard shoulder and came to a halt, trembling like a bare breast in an earthquake.

I didn't know what the hell was happening to me. I'd never had a panic ambush, let alone a full-blown attack. I didn't even know what a panic attack was, because, until then, I'd never had one, or seen anyone else have one.

If you've ever had one, you'll know that anxiety attacks are not made up.

They are not attention-seeking flusters to make girls look more interesting at cocktail parties.

A panic attack is a horribly real and usually terrifying sequence of psychological and physical events triggered by thoughts or situations that the sufferer is often either completely unaware of, or never used to be affected by. They can happen to men, women, children, dogs (yes, dogs) and cranberry muffins (no, not cranberry muffins), and can strike at any age.

A sudden onset of panic disorder happens to thousands of formerly not-panicky-at-all-thank-you people during some kind of existential, midlife wobble.

Or just in the normal course of negotiating the Middle Years.

When mine were at their peak, they made my life a complete misery for about eight years, and had a huge impact on my everyday life, both at home and at work:

I cancelled important work opportunities because I didn't feel able to get on a train (I've even got on a train and then jumped off it seconds before it left, terrified that I might have a panic attack somewhere near Hitchin. I've never been to Hitchin, but it strikes me as the kind of place I might have a panic attack); I spent most of my annual income on taxis because I was suddenly too claustrophobic to even take the escalator down to the Underground, let alone stay on the platform long enough to actually get *on* the thing. My family was forced to sit in a cramped car for HOURS so we could go on holiday abroad without flying; and because I couldn't drive any more either, my then husband had to do the whole 10,000 miles of Autobahn himself; I once wet myself crossing the Millennium Bridge in London because when I got to the middle I suddenly became terrified of the height and the overwhelmingly claustrophobic, agoraphobic, vertiginous nature of having to stay on this tiny, wobbly line, and suddenly thought I was going to jump off; I travelled the entire length of the Severn Bridge crouched on the floor of the passenger seat with a blindfold, crying, 'Oh God oh GOD! Are we nearly there?? Are we nearly there??'

In front of my children.

At its worst, I couldn't even go to the Co-op across the road to buy bread, because the 200 yards between me and the shop just seemed so, so FAR that I couldn't breathe or see or control my fingers enough to dial home and ask someone to come and fetch me.

Eight million people in the UK currently suffer from an anxiety disorder. I reckon another 14 million are in denial. I understand this – it's scary. It feels as if we might be going mad – and as if we might lose everything if we admitted it.

This, in itself, is the madness. We have to talk about. And

as soon as you do, you'll see that you're one of millions feeling the same.

Thirteen per cent of the population is having some kind of panic or anxiety wobble right now. (Absolutely NO idea where I got this stat from, but I'm going with it.)

The guy next to me in the café where I'm writing this is probably staving off inner anxiety right now. The girl in the window having what looks like a first date? I can feel the panic and social anxiety rising from here.

It's as common as stomach bloating before a Christmas do, and it hits LOADS of us in the Middle Years.

I've recently had a flare-up, after a few years of extreme emotional stress, and it's brought it all back again. But that's OK: I know what it is, I know who to talk to, and where to get help.

Counselling, talking therapy and CBT can all have brilliant results. So can drugs, if you need to take that route.

Whatever works, please know and believe that you don't have to be crippled by anxiety and panic disorder the moment your kids get old enough to pronounce it. It CAN be managed. And it's very common at this stage of life.

Sandwich Filler

What follows is an excellent sandwich analogy, but it only works if you're imagining proper sarnies with bread on the top *and* the bottom.

None of your fancy Skandi open-plan ones with fresh salmon piled high, and a pretty little green garnish.

The Middle Years is the full, DOUBLE-CARB gob-stopper. And we are the squashed, dried-out, tasteless, manky tuna in the middle.

Just to be clear.

***

For many of us, our long-awaited 'me-time' is double trashed in the Middle Years, because not only are we still caring for our children, we suddenly ALSO have to look after our elderly parents, grandparents or other members of our family who might need it now.

It's exhausting beyond measure to be the nurse, mum, carer, moral support, financial crux, counsellor, cleaner, taxi service and punch bag for what seems like every single member of the family – and often our partner's family as well – and it can become almost unmanageable at times.

But for a lot of us this is exactly what happens, as parents age, long-term or serious illness strikes, and the burden of care falls to us.

From what I've gleaned, the most important thing to help you survive this truly shattering time is that boring, simple, seemingly impossible thing, of MAKING TIME FOR YOURSELF.

To force yourself to add a layer of self-care into that crushing sandwich of duty and responsibility.

If YOU crumble, the whole thing will fall apart and make an almighty mess on the family floor. No pressure…

So, do whatever it takes to make sure you get some love and care too, even if from yourself and even for ten minutes a day. A bath. Listening to one song you love, some stretching, looking at a magazine you love, watching a 5-min YouTube video of something you like, or just breathing slowly.

Whatever it is that revives and feeds YOU, do it.

Be that tuna, and be the best tuna you can be.

(If you're vegan, then be the best falafel.)

One day you'll be an open Skandi sarnie – and you'll really miss that bread on top.

Breaking Up and Breaking Down

If your relationship comes to an end in the Middle Years – as, let's face it, happens to a lot of people, for a million reasons – it can, and pretty obviously always does, have a massive effect on your mental health. And almost never in a good way, at least initially.

It doesn't matter how old we are, or how much we want or need it, a break-up is almost always emotionally battering.

The end of first love in primary school? Devastated.

Teenage heartbreak? My life is *over*.

First long-term relationship that was THE ONE and then turns out to be... not the one? Train wreck.

But in the Middle Years, after SO much time together, so many years and memories and shared children and mutual friends and responsibilities and habits and routines and small comforts and the creeping realisation that you're not exactly twenty-five any more... splitting up can smash our minds to pieces.

Even if you want out of it.

Even if you don't like the other person.

Even if you are better off without them.

Even if you are the one to call time on it all.

Even if you end up with the house, the kids and the giant pension.

And especially if you end up with none of it.

Not only are your children pulling away from you slowly, but you've now also lost the person you once shared your life with.

And loved.

So, if you don't handle it like a trooper, all 'I GOT THIS!' and keeping your shit together, that's OK.

You go right ahead and fall apart. Lose your fucking mind.

Go insane for a while.

Because any sane person would.

Occasionally though, it's so hard that it's TOO hard to handle.

So, we don't… and then this can happen:

Total Breakdown

Not long after my marriage came to an end – I mean actually ended, officially between the two of us, head to head, as opposed to in all other ways, which it had *many* years before – I had a nervous breakdown.

Since then I've written, shared and talked about it quite a lot, because I'm THAT self-obsessed and narcissistic, but also because I thought it might genuinely help others to know what it is, what to look out for, and, possibly, how to avoid it in the first place.

Every time I've spoken or written about it, I've received an overwhelming response from others who have been through a very similar experience, or think they might be heading for it, and who tell me they are very glad I shared my experiences.

So, narcissistic little me is going to write about it again here, at the risk of boring THE HELL OUT OF YOU, and in case it helps anyone else.

Breakdowns don't tend to just HAPPEN. They creep up.

Mine had been building, slowly, gradually, relentlessly over about a decade, and possibly longer than that.

As my midlife life gathered pace and gnawed away at my marrow, many aspects of my life, or the aspects that brought me fulfilment, confidence, happiness, joy and so on, became increasingly reduced and reduced, until finally almost absent. Many other aspects of my life became ever more exhausting and generally stressful, and unhappy-making; I ignored it all, because that's what most of us do.

Cracks formed.

I carried on.

Gaping holes formed.

I carried on.

Canyons full of cracks formed.

I started to crack. But I carried on.

And then it happened.

Everything I had kept going for had disappeared.

Everything stopped.

And I cracked in half.

I wish I'd known what it was.

I wish I'd seen it coming.

I wish I'd known how to avoid it.

And I wish I'd known how long it was going to take to get over it. (This last one is a REALLY important point, by the way. Almost everyone I know who has a breakdown misjudges how quickly they will be 'back to normal' again. It usually takes about five years.)

Like most of us, I'd heard the term 'breakdown' many times. But I didn't have a clue what it actually meant.

Basically, after receiving a phone call bearing yet another piece of bad, shocking news, I couldn't move.

I couldn't speak, walk, or do anything.

I had to be carried out of the café where I had taken the call, and put on a bench, like a car-crash dummy, motionless and making a strange moaning noise, rocking to and fro, and unable to see anything. A friend waited with me, until my fingers, limbs and body uncurled and unlocked enough to be able to stagger home.

In the weeks and months that followed I spent a lot of time in this state, and learned that's 'catatonic': unable to move or respond to anything.

Staring at the rim of a glass for an hour, tracing the edge of a doorway or a crack on a wall with my eyes, hours spent sitting in a tight little ball of fear, rocking, fingering the corners of my sleeve, trying not to move the molecules of air around me.

I just. Couldn't. Move.

To show the world how OK and 'totally able to look after my children and hold down a job I desperately need, thank you' I was, I had to drag myself off the floor every day and try to fake an outwardly coping persona.

This 'keeping face' worked just long enough to fool the

world, but inside I was so ripped to shreds I found it hard to carry on at all.

Over the next days, and several years, the breakdown continued to show itself in myriad unpleasant ways. I experienced such physical pain in my joints, bones and blood, I often could hardly bear it. I used to cry out from the pain that shot through me without warning, and often when I seemed totally fine. I was often unable to eat or sleep. I had severe night-sweats where rivers of salty fear would pour down my cleavage, arms, legs and stomach, pooling in my tummy and in the gaps between my shoulder bones.

A crab could've made a nice rock pool home in there. I soaked through the entire bed every night, waking in a freezing pool of terror.

I had heart palpitations, blinding headaches, 'explosions' in my eyeballs that left me limp, confused and unable to talk, and full-body spasms that looked like epilepsy.

I didn't know what the heck was wrong with me.

I thought I had mega-flu. Or possibly the bubonic plague.

I did all the usual jazz of going to my GP, and told her I felt down, tired and hopeless, and mentioned the minor matter of my twenty-three-year relationship ending, and the financial and personal stress I was under.

Twelve vials of my aching blood were sent away to the 'Laboratory For The Knackered', to be tested for everything, including self-pity and weakness.

I remember desperately hoping they would find something physically wrong with me. ANYTHING other than the dreaded Mental Health Issue, to account for this horrendous state of being.

But no. My doctor declared this to be a case of Classic Nervous Breakdown caused by chronic, extreme stress.

I needed help, support, medication, therapy and… time.

Lots of it.

She also told me I was totally, absolutely NORMAL to have broken under so much strain.

I think just knowing that was possibly the best medicine of all.

The good news is that it CAN get better.

The bad news is that I think once you've had this experience, you are more vulnerable to it happening again. The nervous system seems to remember what happened, and be quicker to go into it again.

I found this out a few years later – but that's all for another book.

But at least I do know now what breakdown IS, what the symptoms are, and that my body needs some CALM, some gentle care and some time, possibly some counselling and medication, and it can, and WILL, heal.

RAGE

It's OK to be angry.

It's OK to be really fucking angry.

EVEN IF YOU ARE A WOMAN

The deal that's made over women being angry, though!

My GOD.

Are we still supposed to sit there, knitting bonnets looking demure and pretty while keeping the whole household running, raising humans brilliantly, and being largely unthanked for it?

No. We are not supposed to sit there demurely. We are not supposed to do it all and feel unthanked, and unappreciated. We are bloody well allowed to get ANGRY if we feel it.

Shout, scream, RAGE. Get it out.

Then go and get some bloody help if you need it.

You're not a terrible person for being angry and ragey.

You're in the Middle Years, and you feel BROKEN. And you just need some mending.

THINGS THAT HELP

A GP you like, trust and can confide in

Remember that a GP also has a role just to LISTEN. If you have a good GP they should be willing and happy to do this, and, in moments when you just need a 'third ear', eight minutes of their time can make all the difference to how you are feeling, and how you are coping.

I was reticent and nervous about talking to my GP about some more personal matters, my marriage situation, the nature of my relationship, the true state of my mental health at various times, in case there was a negative impact on my kids in some terrifying 'Mummy has been taken away and locked up in a padded cell in Siberia' kind of a way.

But, in reality, she sat, she listened, and then she stopped being a doctor and became a woman. A mother with children, and life problems of her own. It turned out we shared many of the same issues, and just hearing from a medical professional that she too was fallible and had family problems was a huge relief to me.

The words 'it's really OK, you are normal, and this is a really hard time for you. Don't be scared, if you need any help come and see me any time,' helped enormously.

Drugs

They can work. They don't always, but they can.

I feared them for quite a long time, but I wish I'd taken the mood-stabilisers I was prescribed much earlier than I did.

They helped me. They made everything that had become unmanageable, impossible, crazy and totally out-of-what's-considered-normal, become manageable, possible, calm and normal again.

If you're having panic attacks, there is stuff that can help you through it.

If you're depressed, there is stuff that can help you through it.

If you're just not coping at all with the world, there is stuff that can help you cope again.

And in the bizarre, difficult transition of the Middle Years, we sometimes need it most of all.

Therapy

Maybe not forever. Maybe only for a while. Just as needed.

But when it's needed, GO.

I can't tell people this enough. I can't shout it loud enough. I can't wish more than I do that the National Health Service could offer counselling to every single person out there who needs it, WHEN they need it. It should be part of every single person's life.

THERAPY WORKS.

A good therapist will tell you loads of things you already knew but needed to hear from someone else.

They also help you realise loads of things you didn't. And are better off realising.

If you don't like your therapist, go find another one, until you do.

There is SOMEONE out there who can help.

And quite possibly make the next phase of your life a lot better.

Keep looking until you find the right thing to help you.

The right person. The right place. The right activity. The right THING.

It just has to be the right source, for you.

Everyone is different.

Some people use podcasts.

Some write.

Some read.

Some have a best friend to talk to.

Some have no friends, and are perfectly happy that way, and get the help they need from animals.

Some have no friends nearby, but a thousand close friends online, who support them and help them hugely through their mutual wobbles.

THINGS THAT DON'T HELP

Alcohol

Put simply, I can't drink in my forties like I used to in my twenties. Or even thirties.

My body doesn't like it. And my mind doesn't like it either.

It can affect me in some pretty unpleasant ways now – both while I'm drinking, and afterwards.

I get angry, panicky, irrational, aggressive, my attention span goes all over the place, I make bad decisions and pretty much become a nightmare to be around.

This doesn't happen to everyone, but lots of parents I know in the Middle Years got to a point of deciding to STOP.

Maybe not completely, or forever, but certainly to have a bit of a reset of the booze dial. And not one of them regrets it.

Mine got completely out of control for a while during a very (very very very very) stressful period, to the point where I think I was properly addicted.

It took HIM giving up, for me to realise how much I'd been quietly putting away, just to cope with the stress of everyday life, and to numb things a little.

I stopped completely for a month or two, felt horrific to start with (which told me more than enough!) and then went back to it in a much more careful, low-key, Middle Years way.

Caffeine

One double-shot cappuccino is enough for me these days. Despite knowing this, I always have two, and then immediately feel sick, dizzy, anxious and all-round terrible, have a massive energy crash three hours later, and swear I'll never drink coffee again.

Until I do it all again the next day.

This caffeine intolerance came as something of a blow to my already almost non-existent list of naughty luxuries, because I LOVE coffee, I love the café culture, and I like the buzz.

But there it is. I can't drink as much coffee as I used to, and I've had to adjust.

If other people are still knocking back the double espressos, you let them.

If they can handle the caffeine jolt, that's fine.

If you can't, don't. It's just a shift of your midlife body chemistry, and it's best to OBEY.

A Few More 'Self' Things I Wish I'd Known

YOU DON'T HAVE TO GET ON WITH YOUR PARENTS

You don't even have to LIKE your parents.

And your parents don't have to like you, or your life, or anyone in it, or any decisions you make.

It's YOUR life.

The stronger your bond can be with yourself, the happier and healthier your life can be – both for yourself and for your children.

WE HAVE NO CONTROL OVER HOW OTHER PEOPLE BEHAVE, OR HOW THEY FEEL

Realising that they are NOT US, feel differently to us, will receive and understand, process and respond to what we say and do differently to us, is part of understanding who they are – and who we are.

We can't expect anything of anyone. We can hope, wish, ask gently, think they should do X or Y. But we can't expect anything. People do what they do. To expect is to see the world through our own eyes, and, often, to be let down by our own self-centred point of view.

WE HAVE NO CONTROL OVER WHAT HAPPENS TO INFORMATION ONCE WE'VE SHARED IT

If only you know something, then only you know it.

You can hold it, and keep it safe. You can look at it from time to time, see if it's changed – or your view of it has.

It's yours, and yours only, to know AS YOU know it.

But as soon as one other person knows it, you've let it go. Like a dandelion puff, blown into the wind. And from there, it can go anywhere. Land anywhere, be caught by anyone, and seen in a million different lights.

Choose which information to send into the wind, and which to hold onto forever.

THERE IS NO 'WINNING'

Nobody in life really 'wins' anything.

There's so much noise now about winning it, nailing it, smashing it, crushing it, generally kicking the ass out of everything, all in order to WIN!

Sometimes, in the quest to always win, we actually lose out on a lot of other things that are worth far more.

It's nice to win. But it's OK to just let go, stop smashing

and crushing and nailing things, and just enjoy what you already have.

DECIDE WHO YOU WANT TO BE

Think about who you would like to *be*.

What would you like to be *doing*?

Then have a look at who actually you are and what you're doing. Now. Today.

If the two don't match, try to make some small changes every day, until they do. Or at least, until they get a little closer to each other. Small, simple changes can bring about pretty dramatic improvements to your happiness that you might have thought were impossible.

BE WHO THE FUCK YOU ARE

You don't have to like people.

You don't have to like cooking.

You don't have to like eating.

You don't have to drink alcohol.

You don't have to love your curves.

You don't have to trust people.

You don't have to like or do anything that anyone else likes or does.

You CAN like being fit.

You CAN like not doing any exercise, ever.

You CAN like being fat.

You CAN like being thin.

You CAN like going to bed early.

You CAN dislike coffee.

You CAN like posting anything you want on social media, even if it's of no relevance or interest to anyone else.

You CAN have a mental health problem.

You CAN not function properly sometimes.

You CAN decide to keep that private. Or you can share it all.

It's up to YOU.

You can be who the fuck you are. Because if you're not you, then who the fuck are you?

YOU ARE ALLOWED TO FEEL WHAT YOU FEEL

If you're in a beautiful place, and everything is wonderful and you have everything you want and need, and yet you feel sad and empty and unhappy, that's OK.

Don't feel guilty about it. Don't start to tell yourself to 'appreciate the small things' and smell the grass and listen to the birds and be grateful for what you DO have, and write your 'gratitude list'.

Sometimes that works, yes.

But sometimes you just feel shit and low and sad. Feeling GUILTY about not being more grateful or appreciative or in tune with all the good in your life makes it worse.

You feel what you feel.

And you're allowed to feel really sad and lost even if you

have healthy children and a job that pays some bills and a dishwasher and extravagantly soft bath towels.

YOU DON'T HAVE TO BE HAPPY

We live in a time where Being Happy is almost a legal requirement to get a passport.

It's a mark of being a proper person, a real human who has 'found themselves', and is at one with their own soul.

Well, guess what? It's OK to be someone who is basically quite sad, or at least not overtly happy, all the time.

Some of us just don't go around feeling constantly happy, and it's not because we are inherent failures at life or are miserable cunts who should be kept in a sealed container off the coast of Norway or shouldn't have kids.

We are just people who are not SUPER HAPPY ALL THE GODDAM TIME.

And that's OK.

BUT... YOU ARE ALLOWED TO BE HAPPY!

All the above being true, if you are sad ALL the time, or are unable to feel joy, or lightness, any sensation of positivity or mirth, humour in the ridiculous or a sense of pleasure when the first rays of sun touch your skin in May, if you don't feel you are entitled to happiness, don't deserve to laugh and smile at the mundane or everyday, don't feel able to show the world that you ever feel HAPPY, then perhaps you might like to get a second opinion on whether you are OK, and if there might be something you could do to let a little light and happiness back in.

I spent years denying myself happiness, thanks, in part, to a nurturing mixture of underachievement-guilt and hardcore work ethic, to the point where I stopped being *able* to feel happy. Happy equalled lazy, self-indulgent, lazy, guilty, lazy.

This was a huge waste of potential happiness, and good times. If you can't be happy, please find a way to allow yourself this again. Even a little bit happy.

Because a little bit grows into a bigger bit, and, with time, your body and mind can learn that feeling again until it becomes a little part of you, and shines both out, and inwards, again.

And that's a nice feeling – for you, and for those around you.

WE ARE EVERYTHING THAT'S EVER HAPPENED TO US

Even as adults, we are every day of our childhoods.

We are every argument with our parents.

We are every bollocking by our teachers.

We are every exam success and failure at school.

Even as a forty-five-year-old woman, I am still the seven-year-old girl who had her scarf thrown into a rubbish bin outside her classroom, and then trampled on.

Even as a writer and broadcaster with four books and four children to my name, I'm still the fifteen-year-old with braces and acne who took her jumper off too fast on the school bus and her boob fell out.

We carry these things with us throughout our lives. It's easier and healthier to learn to live WITH them, not be burdened by them – and not pass this weight on to our own children.

SAY YOUR SORRIES

Say them, mean them, know what you mean by them, know if you REALLY mean them or not, feel them, live them, deliver them and learn from them.

And then move on.

If somebody won't listen to or accept your sorries, that's ON THEM, not you.

I have hurt people, lied and been unkind. It doesn't matter that I was a broken person at the time. Or that I wasn't being the best me I could be, as a result. It still happened. I was the person I was, and my behaviour was what it was.

But I have realised it, faced it, paid my dues and said my sorries to all who would listen. And I have moved on.

It's all we can do.

If other people can't move on too, can't accept your sorries, and want to remain angry and vengeful and hateful, that's for them to deal with.

We have a right to say sorry for our misdoings, forgive ourselves, and be free.

DE-FRIEND

If someone makes you edgy, unsure, nervous, sad, angry, hurt, not as happy as you might otherwise be… you might be better off without them.

I am terrible at this, but I've learned to get better at it, and it's definitely had a positive impact on my life.

Just CLEANSE.

Delete.

Unfriend.

Block.

Forget.

Life really does go on without them, and, if they were bringing you nothing positive, you have no space for them in your life. It's busy enough.

LOSE GUILT

Guilt is a pointless energy drain. It helps nobody; least of all yourself.

I am HOPELESS at dropping the guilt.

I feel guilty about EVERYTHING.

I feel guilty when I'm at work. I feel guilty when I'm not at work. I feel guilty for not looking after myself properly, and taking no time to rest. I feel guilty when I DO try and rest, and for taking any potential 'useful/work/achieving/housework' time to try some of that 'self-care' stuff I know I need, and we all need.

But I DO TRY to remember the following:

Guilt does you no good.

Nobody can *make you* feel guilty. The feeling of guilt is up to YOU.

Don't feel guilty for being happy.

Don't feel guilty for not being able to be happy.

Don't feel guilty for not being able to pull yourself out of a depression.

Don't feel guilty for not being 'strong enough'.

Don't feel guilty for needing some help from a professional.

Don't feel guilty for not feeling guilty.

Don't feel guilty for making parenting mistakes. (Making mistakes IS parenting!)

To summarise: FUCK GUILT.

And there you have it.

GET IT DOWN

That thing you SWEAR you'll remember in the morning? You won't. Get it down!

Now. On paper, in a note on your phone, on your forehead, in eyeliner on the bathroom mirror. Just WRITE IT DOWN. Or record it. Use that voice recorder thingy they've kindly put on your phone. Call your gran and leave a message on one of the last remaining landline answerphones still in existence. WhatsApp it to a group chat you don't follow any more but feel can suddenly come in hugely useful as an ideas pinboard. I can't tell you how many dead-cert best-sellers, billion-pound business ideas and Superdrug shopping lists have been lost somewhere between 3 a.m. and breakfast.

Gone. I don't know where these thoughts go, because they are clear as vodka under a full moon at the time. But they go. So hold 'em tight, and record them.

'DEVASTATED' DOES NOT AN ATTRACTIVE FRIEND MAKE

If friendships had a Tinder profile, few people would put, 'Broken, exhausted, cries a lot, wants hugs and sympathy, has very little energy to give any support or sympathy back, I'll take a lot more than I give, and I can talk for five hours without pause about how hard the last few years have been, and can swing literally any subject back to the awfulness of my existence. I will cancel our first seven coffee dates because I'll suddenly be too tired and emotional to come out. Sorry about that. But you understand, right, because… I'm not doing so well right now.'

Eventually, WE need to sort our own shit out.

This is a really hard thing to hear, especially when you're so weak you can't see most of the problems, let alone sort them out. But in the end, it's true.

For several years after my breakdown I blamed everything and everyone for a) causing it and b) not helping me fix it.

I was the victim.

I wanted someone or something else to help ME, support

ME, be The One Thing I Really Needed Which Would Solve My Problems.

To give me the answer I needed.

TO MAKE ME BETTER.

WHERE ARE YOU?! Can't you… HELP me?

No. They can't help. Because in the end, it had to come from me.

And it just had to happen when I was ready.

'READY' DOESN'T MEAN 'READY TO GET TOTALLY BETTER'

It means ready to make just ONE thing better.

Take ONE step.

Ready to make ONE phone call.

Ready to dare.

Ready to be bothered.

Ready to believe in yourself again, and in hope, and in a better way of being.

In my case, it took one WhatsApp message, to a friend of mine.

'Do you know any psychotherapists?'

And that was that. She did know one. She gave me her number, and I called her.

A week later, after one hour of talking and listening to what the psychotherapist said, my life started to turn around – very, very slowly and gradually, but definitely.

She enabled me to change the way I saw and could start to

feel about… well, almost everything that had been worrying and destroying my happiness for years.

Did SHE help me?

Yes.

Did SHE do the work?

A bit, yes.

But the rest had to come from me.

I wish I'd gone to find her earlier.

But maybe I hadn't been ready.

LET GO

Of everything and anything that's holding you back, weighing you down, making you sad, making you angry, causing regrets, stifling your creativity, smothering your happiness, stopping you from being a happier version of you.

Let it all go.

People, things, arguments, memories, missed opportunities, bad decisions, unfair things that happened to you and shouldn't have but did so what are you going to DO about it now?

Let it go.

Mistrust

By the time we hit our Middle Years, most of us have had our trust severely tested in one way or another, and our faith in anything being true put through the wringer.

Playground lies, friends who turn out not to be friends, shifty boyfriends or shitty employers who promise a pay rise and then don't see it through.

HUGE LIES. Breath-stealing OH MY GODS. Deceptions that leave you fighting to stand up, gasping for breath, and unable to see anything beyond a huge, shocked blank.

Whether it's a bullshit-manoeuvre/firing/contract drop from an employer, an estate agent pulling the rug from under our feet before we've even stood on it in the house we'd totally agreed with them was ours and had basically moved into in our mind already and told all our kids we were about to live in – yay!! – or a partner who's been gambling our hard-earned money away behind our back while promising he wasn't, a parent who's been cheating on our other parent, finding out our dad isn't who we thought he was and so on, most of us have our most fundamental trust-foundations obliterated at some point along the bumpy way from twenty to forty.

Often, more than once...

If it happens enough times, we can lose all trust, and, eventually, the *ability* to trust.

We look for problems everywhere, the potential hurt, the hidden lies, the invisible line joining the dots in a word that spells BULLSHIT.

But which often isn't there.

Experience of hurt makes us constantly look for something wrong, prepare for it, live according to that fear, and experience all manner of anxieties and sadnesses about something that might not even exist.

Just because it did exist once. Or twice. Or ten times.

Once bitten, twice shy. Ten times bitten, now fucking terrified.

It's a sensible, understandable safety precaution.

But it destroys all happiness and freedom to LIVE.

I've been trust-fucked so many times I find it very difficult to trust any more.

I don't even trust myself, sometimes.

I get why this is, and sometimes it feels sensible, but it often hampers my life and my possibilities, because I'm unable to let go, enjoy, and not worry about what's true and what's not, all the time.

For a long time, I literally couldn't do anything without

fearing all the bullshit that was OBVIOUSLY going on in the background, while I was blithely believing everything, like some gullible fool.

But here's the thing: if someone is going to lie to you, they're gonna lie to you.

If someone is going to fuck you over, they're gonna fuck you over.

If things are going to go wrong, they will go wrong.

They also might not.

We can't stop all the lies and untruths, prevent all the hurt and learn to trust again, if we're running around trying to avoid every single thing that could go wrong, and pre-empting every single lie or deception that might be out there.

We can't trust by trying to prevent all lies.

We might not ever be able to trust.

And that's OK. We all have the history we have.

But if we can't let go of mistrust, or accept it for what it is, we can never breathe.

I'll be lied to again. Someone will shit on me from on high again.

I can't prevent it.

I can just decide to deal with it better.

Work–Life and Other Imbalances

The Middle Years can be a fantastic stage in our working lives.

(For once, that's not sarcasm.)

Many of us have finally found something we actually like doing, or want to learn how to do, and have got a little more time and confidence to do it, at last. Often, it's a time when people decide this is the moment to strike out and start a completely new career, now that we've met New Us, and realised she actually hates being a history teacher.

BUT…

there are a few bastard hurdles in the way that can throw a curveball into the long grass of spanner-filled metaphors, causing all manner of work havoc and practical complications.

I've been self-employed since I had children, so I can't comment on anything to do with office politics, promotions and so on. But I have picked up a few handy things along the freelance way that apply to a lot of us in the Middle Years…

You Are Never 'Free to Go Back to Work'

'Hello, I'd like a job, please. My children have gone back to school and I am footloose and fancy-free once more to use my brain, earn a living and wear fitted shirts from Zara.'

'Sure. When would you like to start?'

'Umm, I was thinking maybe Monday?'

'Monday would be perfect.'

'Oh, wait no, hang on. Shit, sorry. Sorry for saying shit. Oh God, sorry again. I can't do Monday. Millie has a doctor's appointment on Monday. It's been in the diary for *ages* and I daren't move it. It's her ears. How about Tuesday?'

'Tuesday would also be fine. The hours are nine to five, so if you could turn up at—'

'Oh! I'm so sorry, I can't do that.'

'But those are standard working hours.'

'Yes, no, I know, and I'd LOVE to do those hours, I really would, but it's just... the school run. I have to drop Tom off at eight forty-five, and then Millie has moved to a new school across town – they have special teachers who can help with the ear thing – so I can't get to work until about nine-thirty, assuming the traffic is good and nobody has left anything vital at home that they never mentioned they needed until we turn up at the school gate and I have to dash back and get it.'

'Right. Well, we could be very generous and let you start a bit later, but finish later too. Say, six?'

'Ohhh.'

'Oh?'

'Well, it's just that school finishes at three-fifteen. So, I'd need to leave by three, or ideally a bit before, to make it there on time. Tom has some anxiety issues and gets very upset if I'm late.'

'So, you're asking to turn up late and leave early, and possibly not turn up at all if one of your children has some kind of dental, emotional or ear-related emergency?'

'Yes. I'm a parent, and I'd like to be able to work as well.'

'No.'

This, or a thousand versions of this, is the reality for loads of us in the Middle Years. The school-run years. The parents' evening years.

The JUGGLING years.

We are never 'free to work' because we always have one foot tied to the parenting wheel.

(Is that a thing?)

But we all DO manage. Somehow.

We find mum friends and job-shares and childcare that works, and employers who understand why you can't go to a five-day conference in Miami in the middle of your son's A-levels. There are now 'flexible working' movements and initiatives, such as the #flexappeal campaign spearheaded by working mum-of-two Anna Whitehouse (aka Mother-Pukka), to allow more parents to have a job AND go to the school play.

We make it work. It's just not as easy as we might have thought it would be once they go to school.

Missing: MY JOB

For reasons too obvious to explain to someone as smart as you, many parents – and especially mothers – work freelance.

Self-employed, often in creative industries or running their own businesses from home, enabling them to 'work around the kids.'

('Work around the kids' is code for 'working 19 hours a day in the scraps of time you can find between domestic duties and said kids tramping home at 4 p.m. needing FOOD NOW, losing your professional shit before 10 a.m. and never doing anything as well as you know damn well you could, if you could. Anyway.)

Something very unexpected happened to my work in the Middle Years, just when I was in full flow, released from toddler-dom, and loving it. It also happened to a lot of my friends now also in their Middle Years, so I want to mention it here in case it strikes a chord with anyone else, and helps.

Basically, for no apparent reason I could see between my

tears, work dried up. Employers dried up. Budgets were slashed.

Businesses started folding. Clients stopped paying. Customers stopped buying.

The freelance pool got more and more crowded.

The bank account got more and more empty.

It was a huge shock, at this stage of life.

There we'd been, working away perfectly well, reasonably successfully – or at least with some sense of self-worth/job satisfaction/reward/pride/happiness – where suddenly, silently, we were effectively made redundant.

With no warning. No reason given. And nowhere to GO.

It took me years to realise that's what happened, because if you're self-employed nobody is 'fired', or 'made redundant' – you have no job to be fired FROM. You don't get the sympathy hugs, the cheque or cheese hamper. (I've never had a job, so I don't know how hampery it gets if you lose one.)

Freelancers don't have a job to LOSE. We just don't get any further work. It's stealth-redundancy. But it hurts and damages just as much as the real thing.

Confidence and self-esteem were drowned out by self-doubt, despondency and the ping of yet more emails saying, 'We don't actually have a budget, as such, but it's great exposure'...

YES, because we all know that exposure pays the rent and council tax.

Seriously, fuck off with that work-for-exposure crap. Do

you pay your plumber with a mention on Insta stories when he re-plumbs your bathroom? No.

We get paid in actual money, thank you, because it's our JOB. Or, it was.

Because we self-employed types are determined, feisty little sods, we quickly tried to re-learn, re-train, re-group, re-ANYTHING to keep up with the huge changes required to survive in a world now dominated by likes, RTs and followers.

We became our own agents, PR gurus, sales and marketing executives and contract lawyers. We mastered selfies and advertising campaigns, learned about clickbait and memes, publicity strategy and sales techniques.

We got to know the hashtag for everything and the meaning of nothing.

It was a contradictory and confusing decade of ever more opportunities to succeed... and to fail.

Fast, hard, and mentally crushingly.

I've read reams of tear-filled accounts from other self-employed mums in the 'prime' of midlife, of commissions chased, secured, completed and then dropped – unpaid – for no reason; of years of professional let-downs as hardworking people with skills and experience were picked up and dropped without explanation; of professional promises made, on which important family financial decisions were based, only to have them dashed in one blunt, impersonal, terminal email, leaving us with no way of paying for the school trip to

Normandy or Lego obsession, and feeling… well, shit, quite honestly.

We take on emergency childcare to finish a job with an Urgent Urgent Urgent Deadline of NOW!!!! and stay up all night crying over the three missing quotes the editor INSISTS she needs, and then wake up, exhausted, guilty and tearful the next morning, only to find the job won't come off after all, for reasons never given. And there's no kill-fee.

Suck it up, love. Shit happens.

And the harder it gets, the more we try – anything and everything.

Instagram isn't just about pretty cups of coffee and 'inspirational' quotes. It's an indispensable business tool and marketing platform.

To add to the list of indispensable business tools and marketing platforms we're supposed to have.

Platforms that now throb and buzz and prod us 24/7 in our pockets, thanks to our smartphones (= offices) coming with us on the school run, to piano lessons, parents' evenings and Sunday nights on the sofa.

Every ping and beep could mean… WORK!! A COMMISSION! MONEY! Wait, honey, hang on, Mummy has to check her email NOW and respond NOW or the job might go elsewhere, and… shit. Shit, it's gone. ARGH!

Cue shouts of frustration, blame and rage at the world, a curt snap at a child who just wanted to show you their milk-bottle rocket, and soul-sapping guilt at being a terrible parent who is juggling it all and dropping every ball.

All of this HUGE change and the vertiginous, urgent learning curve to stay in ANY way relevant or part of the party I once enjoyed, got me down. Really, really down.

And, truthfully, I don't think it made me a particularly nice person at all.

I was angry and resentful; hurt and broken. I felt owed and professionally cheated, lost and sad. And fucking exhausted by it.

It just didn't make any sense.

Why, when it was all going so well, was there suddenly no work?!

And why, if there was no work, was I busier than ever, never 'out of the office', constantly on call, beavering away, ignoring my kids, ignoring my husband, obsessing over my 'potential' work… but earning zilch??

Not everyone wants a paid job as well as being an unpaid parent – and that's obviously not only OK, but bloody amazing work. Raising little humans is, after all, the hardest job there is.

But for a lot of us who either *need* to work to bring in the dosh (so… pretty much all of us, then) or who just love working and feel their work is a big part of their identity, independence, freedom and creative fun, struggling to find work, or feeling the Middle Years plate-spinning is just not allowing us to work as we would like to, can have a catastrophic effect on our mental wellbeing.

The gratification, mental stimulation, sense of fulfilment and, frankly, time away from kids and chaos and OMG CAN I JUST THINK PLEASE, can mean the difference between happiness and real depression for a lot of us.

And I really, really struggled with it. I lost my creative joy, a huge part of myself, my freedom and my self-esteem. I lost my way, my integrity, my beliefs and a big part of ME.

I desperately clung to whatever and whoever could offer me the faintest glimmer of a lifeline back into the world of work I loved so much. Whatever would numb the pain of loss of what I HAD, and loved, and didn't understand why it had been taken away.

I made huge mistakes during this time, wasted a lot of time and energy on bitterness and anger, felt things I'd rather not have felt, did things I wish I hadn't done, and learned a lot about my own failings and weaknesses.

To be honest I think I turned into a bitch for a while. Just a horrid, empty being, devoid of any sense of self, purpose or direction. Maybe I felt in some way justified in being a bitch, because the world had shat on me, wasn't giving back. I don't know.

It wasn't my finest hour, and I think it took me years to realise it was very much related to a loss of work.

I wish I'd had a little more counsel and advice around this time about the realities of working in the Middle Years, how to cope emotionally when a career doesn't sky-rocket at the exact moment we think it will, and how to adjust to the new work playing field without lying in the mud, crying.

We can get through it – it just takes a major adjustment in managing our expectations, realities, and bank accounts.

Don't Make Work Enemies

In this day and age of career fickledom, people move jobs a LOT. One day they're copy-editing on a local rag, the next they're the social media coordinator for a brand of vegan condoms, and before you know it they're CEO of a global pharmaceutical industry in New York, or have chucked it all in to set up an online needlework course in Orkney, and are blissfully happy there.

Work enemies have a very annoying habit of moving on into other jobs at the EXACT place you really, really want to work. Often, this is years down the line. In a life you never expected to have, for a job you never thought you'd want.

But there they are. Standing between you and the job you so desperately want, and need.

And you're screwed.

Paying the bills is hard enough as it is, so if you CAN, just smile, hold your head up high, let them have their say, and leave with grace and style… and a paid gas bill.

There are other jobs. For now, avoid telling your bitchy

employer she's a bitch. She IS a bitch. But she doesn't need to hear it from you.

I Hate This Bloody Job. Or... Do I?

Is it really the job, or is it the place you're in yourself? Are you bringing your 'midlife urgh' into the job, and putting the blame for all your stress, anger, exhaustion and hair-loss onto deadlines, annoying colleagues, shit colleagues, stupid colleagues, unfair bosses, unfair pay-grades, unfair Universe... when actually, if you were in a better place in yourself, you'd probably cruise it?

I've quit jobs I had worked and toiled and striven and waited years to get, simply because I wasn't in the right place in myself to do them at the time.

I was in a bad place in my life, I was too unhappy and angry and tired to deal with the world properly, and I blamed everything. Even when there was no fault at all. Or sometimes when there was. But I couldn't deal with it well at the time.

So, I quit.

And regretted it.

I wish I'd had someone to sit down with me and give me

some gentle big-me-up counsel, to talk it through, and to help me keep it going.

I didn't.

So before you quit… make sure it's not just the way you're feeling at this moment, and you don't just need a walk around the block and a good cry.

That said…

If You Really, Really Hate Your Job…

Leave.

There are other jobs. I know loads of people who decided enough was enough, took what felt like a terrifying risk at the time, threw in their towels and aprons and iPads, started a new job… and got a fantastic new lease of life.

They retrained, went back to college, took an evening class, joined an online freelancers' group that led to a first job in writing or cookery or 'content creating' or social media managing or 'zine publishing or accounting or CHRIST KNOWS WHAT.

They did it.

And it was the best thing they've done for years.

Me? Go Back to COLLEGE??

Yes, you. You!!

If you want to do it, DO IT.

Go back to college.

Retrain. Relearn. Restart!

That degree you always wanted in textiles and design? GO GET IT.

That qualification in cookery? It's yours to have.

That creative writing course? Take it.

GO! If not now, then when? When you're seventy?!

Do it now.

At least then you've DONE IT.

I know so many people – especially mothers – who have had total career changes in the Middle Years. Who bit the work bullet, got the funding, spent the evenings editing spreadsheets and writing essays and learning how to use software they'd never heard of a year ago, like a BOSS.

They've changed their whole working lives, minds and incomes. And have loved every second of it.

It's not too late.
Until you're dead, it's never too late.
For anything.

Stop Rushing

We are all in a rush. Everything has to happen NOW! Yesterday! Last month! Quick! Now! Shiiiiit, can't breathe. Time is running out! People are DOING THINGS I'm not. Must do all the things now!

Someone else will do/have/see/write/live what WE should have!

Yes. They might. Maybe they already have.

But that's OK.

There's room for *you* to do it all too.

Especially if you stop rushing.

Work Insecurities

Most of us in our Middle Years still have major work insecurities, and sometimes suffer from crushing imposter syndrome and crises of confidence in the workplace. Even the people who pretend they don't, do.

And that probably won't change.

It starts at nursery when some other kid drew a better picture of a house and a tree, because THEY PUT A BIRD IN THE SKY and they got a sticker.

It grows at school when we're asked about what happened to Mary in *Walkabout*, and even though we've read it five times we suddenly doubt everything we know, in case it's wrong and we look stupid, so we panic and say something wrong and stupid, and everyone laughs.

And this just carries on into the workplace.

There's always the office bitch, the cocky intern, the vile editor, the back-stabbing assistant, the misogynist boss.

Fuck 'em. You are doing JUST FINE. And you're nicer.

PART 3

The Relationships Bit

3a: Staying Together

WHO ARE WE NOW?

When our children stop filling every second of our waking (and sleeping) lives with STUFF THEY NEED US TO DO RIGHT NOW, a weird moment occurs.

Uninterrupted by the constant noise, needs and distracting presence of our kids, we can find ourselves, for the first moment in more than a decade of home life, suddenly standing in the kitchen together, in silence, without having to clear up any football boots or Spanish homework papers or art projects or broken phone covers.

And in that moment, we can suddenly look at the person we've shared over a decade of home life with, and notice the way they are standing, and breathing, what they're wearing now we've actually come to notice it, and how their left arm seems a bit shorter than the other one (is it the sleeve, or the weird arm length?), how they move, and who they ARE, in that moment of silence.

It's the loudest silence we've ever shared.

And we think…

Sorry but, who ARE you?

And… who am I?

What and who and HOW are we, as a couple, as a unit, as lovers, parents, friends… NOW? Now, a decade on. Now, in our lives without babies and toddlers.

Now, as us.

Are we the same people who skipped into the parenting tunnel ten years ago, waving a photo of our twenty-week scan and beaming at all the joy to come – but now just a bit older, more irritated by each other's dental floss habits, and with ever more pubic hair?

Or are we now so changed by everything that followed – by life, work, family, health, people, events, car insurance, disastrous Airbnb apartments in various back alleys of Europe, collagen depletion around the eye and lip area which doesn't seem to respond to that special cream we've used for the last five years, and all the huge Everything Else that's happened while we were both crawling from toddler groups to parents' evenings to work presentations to trips to A&E with a fevered child, and by the simple linear passing of TIME – that… we are just different people now?

(Keep breathing. It's all going to be OK.)

In all likelihood, yes. We are different people now. Of course we are – and one would hope so! If I'm the same person I was when I was twenty-five I'd like a refund on the last twenty years, please.

But if we're both so different now, in our post-early-years awakening, are we still compatible?

Maybe we are, and even MORE so than before. Maybe we like this new forties us even more than drunk, confused twenties us. Maybe it's a fantastic new stage we're going into together, free from looking after kids all the time. Free to be us, enjoy us, travel with us, have sex with us anytime, anywhere, anyhow.

Maybe this, at last, will be our #bestlife?

Or… are we different, but allergic to each other?

Do we detest the very air we breathe? Do we want to garrotte each other with that piece of dental floss that's been abandoned on the bathroom floor for a week? Can we list 475 things that irritate us about the way our partner drinks coffee? Can we bear the fact that the person we met has far less 'matured with age' than… gone well past his best-before date already?

Do we silent-cry while we fuck, which now only happens once every other month and mostly just to be able to tell a lawyer one day that we DID MAKE AN EFFORT, OK?!

This scenario is probably not so #bestlife.

Do we know each other?

Do we know ourselves?

Do we WANT to know any of this?

Should we just go back to unloading the dishwasher and

sorting out that electricity bill, ignore it all and hope that our fabulous fifties will bring on some kind of stupendous and sexually invigorating decade of lust and love?

It's a weird one, that moment you meet your 'new' old partner, sans kids, and see what's left of you each, and you together.

It's like Ultimate Tinder in reverse – a date with the person you've already lived with for fifteen years, and now have to read their new profile – and see if you like it.

It's great if you do.

But OK if you don't. It's really OK.

It's not you, it's just both of you.

Crossroads

I reckon the whole thing about midlife relationship crises isn't about 'crisis' at all.

It's also not particularly about midlife, because it can happen absolutely nowhere near the middle of your life.

So that's all nice and clear so far.

It's more about a midlife… junction.

Midlife realisations.

Midlife crossroads.

And daunting midlife decisions about whether we should go straight ahead, or…

TURN OFF IT. (Which, ironically, we may have already done as regards feelings towards our partner, leading to this messy junction in the first place. Awesome.)

Should we, though?

Should we listen to that overwhelming, panicky sense that if we don't turn off NOW, we might never get the chance again??

Almost every normal, sentient human being with feelings,

thoughts, desires, a sense of wonder at life and all it contains and a still-palpable heartbeat, hits the Middle Years of family life and has some kind of existential, mind-shattering…

IS THIS IT???? moment – and immediately wants to run away from it all, if only to the nearest bar, though possibly also to a bar in Corfu or New York.

Even if everything's going pretty well, the dishwasher isn't broken, your children still speak to each other, you fancy your partner just enough to keep going (or coming), you have something that resembles a job, you can go on holiday once a year to refresh your memory about the joys of sitting in a hot car with children for six hours, and you don't live in a disease-ridden war-zone, it's still plum-normal to think:

'Right, you know what? Fuck this, I've had enough. This is nice enough and everything, but… I want a change. I don't know exactly what I want to change TO, but I just want… SOMETHING ELSE… Something, that isn't this. I want a new start. (And definitely a new middle.)'

Years and years of basically the same road can create a glorious, calming sensation of entrapment, boredom, breathlessness, claustrophobia and that feeling when your skinny jeans get soaked in the rain and you can't get them off because your stupid heel won't get round the clingy fabric and ARGH… GET ME OUT OF HERE!

If you WANT to be on this road, you'll stay. It doesn't matter how worn the tarmac is; you like it there. Just the way it is. Worn bits and all.

You don't want anything else.

But if you *only* feel unhappy, unappreciated, unloved, uncared for, un-nurtured, unsatisfied, unstimulated, unexcited, overworked and under-slept, if you're sleepwalking through what should still be exciting, interesting, ALIVE years of your life, while your body is still functioning roughly as it should, you have dreams and ambitions yet to fulfil, a continent bladder, and still look reasonably nice in tiny black knickers, and if you find yourself wondering ALL the time if there are other, better roads you could be on… you've probably turned onto them already.

And maybe that's OK, and better to know it now, face the truth, make the required decisions, and turn off.

I Hate That Clicky Thing You Do with Your Mouth

Scientists did some sciencey things once, and discovered that the average time for two cohabiting humans to want to kill each other is four and a half days (reduced to eighteen hours when children are introduced into the equation). Given this unquestionable fact, I'd say it's something of a major achievement for anyone to make it into the Middle Years and still not only be in a relationship with the person with whom they produced offspring ten years ago, but also still speak to them civilly.

Somewhere along the long parenting line, Cupid tends to get admitted to A&E with an acute case of Resentment, Irritation and Wandering Eye, and his affliction has a catastrophic effect on many previously perfectly tolerable relationships, making every passionless day feel like crawling towards the marriage gallows, naked, with your bum hairs on fire. All the things you once loved about your partner now make you want to kill them before breakfast.

And that's on a good day.

And thus the big, sad, expensive, exhausting Midlife Relationship Cull commences.

It's often not the Big, Obvious WHAM BAM Things that end long-term relationships. It's the millions of little ones that grow, fester and putrefy over time, and destroy what was once really rather beautiful – especially after a few gin and tonics.

It's forgetting to refill the water filter. Every time.

It's hanging laundry the wrong way, so that the corners don't dry.

It's making the wrong packed-lunch fillings for the children.

It's not writing the music lesson cheques. Or knowing which instruments they play.

It's that clicky thing you do with your mouth when you yawn.

It's tea breath.

It's filing your nails while watching a film together.

It's shouting up the stairs instead of bothering to go up there and talk to me instead.

It's a sigh when someone has forgotten that thing you just told them three times.

It's not putting the carrot peelings into the compost bin straight away.

It's not booking the holiday when it was needed.

It's booking a holiday when it was not needed, and you can't afford it.

It's saying 'yes' to a child's request, when you've just said 'no'.

It's using the wrong tone of voice on the phone.

It's not guessing that when I said, 'I don't want to talk about it' I meant, 'I DESPERATELY NEED TO TALK ABOUT IT.'

It's living with someone for so long that scar tissue has built up around the heart and it can't beat any more.

It's breathing too loudly during a film.

It's not saying 'hello, how was your day?' whether you actually care or not.

It's misreading road maps.

It's leaving the soap in a pool of water.

It's being the favoured parent.

It's huge, built-up resentment of your partner's supposedly 'better' life.

It's deep insecurity, carried forward from childhood.

It's not saying 'I love you' any more.

It's not meaning 'I love you' any more.

It's not kissing any more.

It's forgetting to do all the things we should have remembered not to forget.

No Evenings = No Us

Losing almost all of our available evening time in which we could potentially be together, AS A COUPLE WITHOUT KIDS, was, for me, a hugely unexpected, and, frankly, a pretty devastating change, in relationship terms.

But it happens to most parents.

Because when most of their kids are older than about twelve, they start going to bed AFTER WE DO.

For actual fuck's sake.

Think about this, for a moment.

At the end of every day, when you've worked all day and cooked dinner and washed up and done the laundry and helped with chemistry homework that you couldn't do, and argued with your partner about whether you can bear another Christmas with his family, and put out the recycling bins, and now you just REALLY want to have a hot bath and then sit down on your arse next to the person you love, or think you still love but it's hard to tell as you never see each other any more except to say 'hi' and 'whose charger is this?', and watch something mindless and unchallenging together, or maybe try to be a bit physical or sensual or even urgently shaggable LIKE NOW RIGHT HERE BY THE MICROWAVE, you CAN'T, because two of your children still haven't had a shower yet, one is FaceTiming her mates in the kitchen, another is yet to come back from a street dance class, and the telly is currently being used for an online Fifa match against a kid in Year 8 who lives across town.

It's quite tricky at this point not to scream: 'OHMYGOD CAN WE PLEASE GO BACK TO WHEN THEY WENT TO BED AT 7 P.M??!'

Here's what evenings generally look like in the Middle Years:

Helping one child or other with homework. Because older kids have body clocks that run on Los Angeles time and think 8 p.m. is a perfectly acceptable time to start writing a 1,000-word essay about the key mental health themes of *To Kill a Mockingbird*, and how this related to Harper Lee's own life experiences with her mother.

Sorting out school uniforms. WHY? Why so many shirts? Why so many of them so dirty. Why this happen so fast? Why me no speak English any more?

Collecting a child from some sports thing, music thing, drama thing, friend's thing, after-school thing, after-after-school thing, party thing, committee meeting thing, thing thing. Just when they're FINALLY old enough to make their own way home, they decide to have so much STUFF with them they can't carry it all.

Perfect.

THIS is what's wrong with kids these days: not enough arms.

Sorting out some kind of personal crisis with one of your offspring, whose primary method of therapy seems to involve weeping mascara onto the clean duvet cover and kindly making sure we also have a personal crisis, what with all the child-weeping and mascara situation.

I reckon we managed about one evening in ten when we both managed to be not only present in the same room sans kids, but also not mentally smashed enough by the day to have half a semi-coherent conversation, before we fell asleep.

This loss of evening time is a relationship bitch.

Evenings are when you are Not A Parent Any More. It is when you reconnect with… YOU.

The you that you were before they made you… not you.

The you your partner fell in love with.

The you who fell in love with your partner.

Evenings are also when you spend time doing… nothing.

Mending.

Healing.

Thinking.

Masturbating.

Being silent.

Eating Doritos like nobody's watching. Because nobody is watching.

These moments allow us to be free. To return to ourselves and be childlike and giggly, or calm and reflective. Or, every other Valentine's Day, a little bit sexy with our partner but not until too late please because I've had a long day and I really hate being tired on a work day.

To lose the evenings is to lose the time spent with YOU.

Either you with yourself, or you with your partner.

I LOVE MY EVENINGS. I LIVE for my evenings. Anyone who stands between me, my bath and QUIET TIME risks losing both arms and a month's pocket money. I got so obsessed with hanging on to even the SMALLEST bit of what was left of my evenings that I started to get stressed about it at lunchtime, and it built joyfully throughout the day until I was so tetchy and wound up at dinner about the imminent annihilation of My Time, most people in my house just wanted to get away from me as fast as possible.

Which was the whole idea, I guess.

I still lament the loss of those blissful Early Years evenings, when the children were tucked up in bed after a nice 6 p.m. bath and a rendition reading of *The Gruffalo*, with all the voices, like a piña colada misses a cocktail umbrella.

I never really thought about this happening, until it did.

You do GET those evenings back again, but usually not until the children leave home and the house is so eerily empty and abandoned we wish them back again.

***

NOTE: evening conversations in the Middle Years are almost only ever about admin, kids, work, more admin, admin the other person hasn't done, admin we have to do and WHY IS IT ALWAYS ME??, other people's kids, our own parents, school admin, bills, Bill's admin, and why Instagram algorithms are now so shit. Talk about something else.

Talk about SOMETHING ELSE. Please. Before you forget how to.

***

Further Very Important Note on talking:

If you have ONE uninterrupted conversation per week with your partner in The Middle Years, of *any* kind and lasting more than 18 seconds, you're doing miles better than the rest of us.

What I Say; What I Mean

'I don't want to talk about it.'

I really need to talk about it.

***

'I need to talk about it.'

Don't even THINK of mentioning it.

***

'No, no, that's fine. I'll pick them up. IT'S FINE.'

I will NEVER let you forget that I did this, and I will mention it every day for the next eight years.

***

'Lunch with your parents on Sunday would be great.'

IN WHOSE LIFE????

***

'Does my bum look…'

This is so obviously NOT about my bum, but about 700 other things that are currently upsetting me, and you need to work out what they are. In a nanosecond.

***

'All you have to do is say "you look nice".'

You're only saying I look nice because you know you're supposed to say that.

***

'Can't you ever just ask me about my day?'

If you get the tone wrong, I'll know you don't mean it.

***

'I think you look lovely clean-shaven.'

OMG WHERE HAS YOUR BEARD GONE?? Is this what your FACE actually looks like?

***

'I fancy a quiet night in.'

I am GAGGING to go out.

***

'I think I'll have a hot bath tonight, relax, do a face-pack, you know, just chill. OK?'

I don't want to talk to you. And I have something I want to watch on my phone.

***

'It's OK, I'll do it.'

Why the FUCK do you never do it?

***

'I'm fine, really.'

I'm about to have a breakdown.

***

'What do YOU think?'

Please think exactly what I think, or we'll have to have an argument about it and I'm too tired.

***

'Can't you ever just agree with me?'

Why don't you just say what YOU want, so I know?

***

'Why don't you just say what YOU want, so I know?'

Only tell me what you want if it fits with my plans for what I want.

***

'I'm just really hormonal right now.'

I feel sad and I'm using hormones as the reason because you CANNOT dispute this or do anything except feel sorry for me and not be able to empathise in any way, so just HUG ME.

Arguments

The Middle Years are the PEAK time for arguments between parents, because we've now amassed at least ten years of things to argue ABOUT, and it's all built up like a giant, pulsating boil engulfing us in a heady mix of hatred and resentment.

It's beautiful.

Also, most of us have given up trying to be nice.

Our twenties are for nice.

Our thirties are for wondering just how far this 'nice' thing is really getting us.

Our forties are for… yeah fuck it, I'm done. JUST WIPE YOUR SHAVING FOAM OFF THE BASIN AND YOUR PISS FROM THE UNDERSIDE OF THE TOILET SEAT, WILL YOU?!

In the early stages of a relationship, arguments pop up every few days, last thirty-five seconds and then it's all… I'm sorry, I love you, here, take your knickers off I want to fuck you in the sink.

In the Middle Years, when your house is full of moulting teenagers leaving used sanitary pads on the toilet floor and spraying spots onto the bathroom mirror, you have… a little less inclination/opportunity/fuck-giving towards the whole fuck-having thing.

You just want an argument.

In general, there are only two points you want to make, which win all arguments at this stage of life:

Your life is so much easier than mine because you don't look after the kids AND work

and

Why can't you be more like me, because I do things better?

That's pretty much it.

You can go round and round the houses, with logic and reasoning and fairness and yada yada yada.

But basically, it all boils down to:

You're a lucky bastard, and I am right.

Why? Because I grew our children in my body and gave birth to them.

I WIN FOREVER.

There's a maximum number of times you can use this line effectively, because he has literally NO comeback from it, so it's a little harsh to just keep using it over and over.

I would suggest this number is 750,000.

This means, if you are married for twenty years, you can use it 102 times a day.

***

These days there seems to be much enthusiasm among parents for sharing their marital strifes with their kids.

Bringing it all out into the open, being all HONEST with them about everything.

To this I say… no. Just Jesus, no.

First up, they are *children.* Adult relationship issues are not really part of a child's domain. Or shouldn't be.

Much as we might think it's all contemporary and hip to SHAAAAARE everything… it's not.

Secondly, they're not stupid. They know when their parents are not getting along.

All that shouting, sighing, crying, spitting through gritted teeth and smashed crockery are fairly solid indicators of things being not entirely rosy, that even semi-aware children can spot a mile off, from as early as the age of one. Yes really.

Sharing the finer details of *why* Mummy is crying every night, why Daddy spends so much time alone in the bathroom, and who 'Susan' is, is to bring them into a world they can't possibly understand, nor should, and will only serve to make them hate either one or both of their parents.

And definitely Susan.

And, worst of all, possibly themselves. Children often blame themselves for problems their parents are having, and this can have life-long consequences. Try to let them know that you're sorry things are a bit stressful right now, but it's nothing at all to do with *them*, and they've done nothing wrong.

If they want to talk about it, let them.

If they want to ask questions, let them.

If you answer them, be selective.

Oh, and…

Don't. Slag. Each. Other. Off.

We all know we should never slag our partner off in front of our children.

It's damaging, unfair, cheap, low, divisive… and almost unavoidable when you're really hacked off.

So, we all do it.

There MAY have been occasions when I was at home, just idling around trying to write an article to a tight deadline while looking after our children while filing a tax return while hanging out six loads of washing while cooking while SOMEONE ELSE was just… not there, when I'd lose my resolve and break into a fun game of… OH, AND WHERE IS DAD?

It's like those lift-the-flap board books for kids, where you have to find Spot. (Who is always under the stairs, by the way. The smart kids cut straight to the last page, roll their eyes at you, and then go off and read a better book.)

Where is Dad?

Is he cleaning the fridge? No, he's not.

Is he making your toast? No, he's not doing that either.

Is he folding away 700 pairs of socks that don't match? Nope.

Maybe he's filling in your GCSE options with you that were due yesterday? No?

Oh, wait a minute. What's this???

Dad is... IN HIS CLEAN, AIR-CONDITIONED, FREE, STATIONERY-FILLED OFFICE, with superfast Wi-Fi and free coffee and a biscuit tin that gets refilled by someone else.

Just there, all on his own... working. With nobody pestering him about whose turn it is on the Xbox or covering his desk in Lego or shouting at him to bring up new toilet paper.

THAT'S WHERE DAD IS. THE SUPERHERO.

This is usually the point where I realise I'm being a Grade A Bitch, I feel horrible about myself, I know my children also think I am horrible, and now they like Dad way more than me.

And damn right, too.

So, I vow never to do it again.

Until tomorrow.

Sarcasm

Lowest form of wit, apparently.

Also, highest form of twattery in a domestic row.

When we're having an argument and I use sarcasm, put on a baby voice and repeat what he just said, I know the evening is done for.

I also know I'm being a pathetic child and just need some fresh air, and an hour to let it blow over.

Go Away. I Need A Hug

Sometimes we push everyone away, when what we crave is closeness.

We make ourselves unlovable, when all we want is to be loved.

We know we're doing it. We hate that we're doing it. And that makes everything worse.

I do it. I close off completely and build a shell of fire around me that burns anyone who comes within striking distance. Often the shell of fire is surrounded by an electric fence too, for added welcoming effect.

I usually do this fire-rejection thing when I'm feeling down, and all I need is closeness. It's so stupid, but I do it; because I'm so closed off or sad or angry or troubled in myself, within my electric ring of sadness, I don't know how to HAVE closeness.

I only know how to create distance.

So I do.

And I watch it. And I hate it.

So I do it more.

I think my marriage started to fall apart because of a beautiful combination of massively unresolved childhood emotional issues (still present... but working on it at last IN MY FORTIES. Go me), sadness, anger, exhaustion, self-hate projected as hate of others, hanging out with assholes, making myself as dislikeable as possible, especially to myself, and sitting there all on my own, burning in my fire-pit and throwing out flames every so often. Like, every day.

I still occasionally do it now, but at least I'm aware of it, I KNOW I'm doing it, and I've learned to try to register it, look at it head-on, and stop it.

No 1 strategy here is to send some kind of message, cunningly in the form of a message, that says:

I NEED TO BE CLOSE BUT I CAN'T DO IT.

CAN YOU PLEASE DARE TO COME CLOSER, BELIEVE I WON'T BURN YOU, AND HOLD ME TIGHT SO I CAN STOP PUSHING YOU AWAY?

And that almost always works.

Knowing Me Knowing You

Know your partner in good times.

Know your partner in bad times.

Know yourself in good times.

Know yourself in bad times.

Know what you both need. And don't.

That might not be the same for you both.

Neither is right, or wrong. It's just different.

And knowing that, can make all the difference.

Silence, or a talk?

Distance, or a hug?

To be shouted at, or listened to?

Tough love, or gentle support?

Pushed harder to deal with the challenges they face, or wrapped in cotton wool until they're ready?

Challenged, or just agreed with for now, even if you disagree, just because they need that right now?

Fuck, though, humans are complicated, aren't we?!

And all different.

In Health... and in Sickness

The Middle Years can be the first time we've had to deal with major un-wellness – not just in ourselves, but in our partners.

I say 'un-wellness', because it's not really the same as 'illness'.

It's just... not-WELLness.

This not-wellness can take many forms, but often it's mental or emotional, and comes as the result of a build-up of decades of pressures, stresses and sadnesses, never-addressed childhood grievances or emotional upsets, professional disappointments and internal personal struggles, finally coming to the fore.

Major periods of depression, anxiety, chronic neck or back pain from work or just good ol' ageing/wear-and-tear (which, helpfully, can often cause depression as a result of the pain and inability to do things 'normally' any more), creeping and now problematic addictions or destructive habits, loss of self-esteem, some kind of breakdown, crisis or other not-wellness – whatever it is, the Middle Years are often the time when they decide to show themselves, and it can come as something of a grenade to the stability of a family.

JUST at the time you were looking forward to having time to be 'a couple' again.

There's a whole book to be written about this (OK *fine*, I'll write it) but for now it's enough just to say that this is very common, and it's not a sign of failure or disaster.

If you can work through it – together or separately, whichever works best for you both – and you find support networks and professional help, you can not only 'get through it', but you can emerge stronger and better together than you were before.

Then the Later Years can be some of the best you've ever had.

No, it's not easy. Yes, it's exhausting and unexpected and about the last bloody thing you need right now!

But with love, compassion, patience and faith in what you DO have, it's totally possible.

The Lives of Others

Relationships between ourselves and the ones we love are complicated enough already, without letting the entire world wade in with their conflicting opinions as well.

These days, twitching net curtains have been replaced by twitching tweets, prying WhatsApps and stinging Instagram DMs.

I used to get really knocked down by external voices who suddenly decided it was their right to offer their opinions about things in my life they didn't understand because they weren't on the firing line.

Many times in my bumpy Middle Years I wanted to scream and shout 'but you don't KNOW ANYTHING ABOUT THIS!' at them, through my phone. Which, weirdly, rarely helps.

Now, slowly, I've learned to ignore it all, and remember that people just like to vent their opinions – we don't have to listen to them or be affected by them. What happens in any family is what happens in THAT family. Your family. Your relationship. Your life.

And that goes as much for the way we might comment on and judge OTHERS, as well.

Other people's lives are nobody's business but that of the people immediately involved. And only those people. Not everyone in the entire community who knows nothing about any of the complicated details, but only what they've gleaned through spin-whispers and Facebook messages.

Everyone bar the people directly involved in your situation can fuck their nosey gossiping faces right off and keep their sighs and tutting to themselves.

Other people's lives are always far more complicated than any one of us knows, needs to know or has any business knowing.

The only people who need to deal with a painful, personal family situation, hurt through it, apologise, forgive and mend after it, are the people directly involved. Not his mates. Or her girlfriends. Or their wider family. Or their Instagram following.

Someone else's personal life is nothing to do with us. Our personal life is nothing to do with anyone else.

If apologies are due, make them to the people who are owed them. If dues are to be paid, pay them to the people who are owed them. If consequences are in order, see them through.

Then move on.

Under the Influence

When we are in turmoil and don't know which way to turn, most of us seek some kind of advice – from a family member, a counsellor, or, most often, a friend.

This is all very sensible, so far. But, it comes with a warning: every person's advice is massively influenced by their own situation, history and character. Whether it's relevant, helpful or even kind to you or not.

Friends who are in long-term marriages that they believe in, who have weathered a few major storms and made it work, who believe in the stability of family life and a bit of give and take on all sides will probably say everything to encourage you to stick with it, and try to make things work.

Friends who've recently come out of a dreadful relationship might encourage the end of yours.

Those who were never really very committed to their partner and thought it was OK to sleep around with anyone and everyone, despite being in a solid, long-term relationship, may well 'YOU GO GIRL' you towards the idea of randomly shagging some guy from work, and you'll feel much better. You might not. You might feel a LOT worse.

Depending on who you talk to, cry on and drip snot over, you can find yourself in a dizzying mental flip-flop between 'yes, I should stay' and 'no, I should go' for months.

The thing with being in troubled waters is that you think you're drowning. Consequently, if someone throws you something, *anything*, to cling onto you'll grab it with both hands and hang on as if your life depended on it. Because it does.

And sometimes we grab the wrong stick, the wrong advice, the wrong counsel, just because it's there.

When we're vulnerable, we can be easily influenced – for good and for bad. By people, by films, by song lyrics, by something we hear on the radio, by a podcast, by someone sitting next to us in the park who just looks happier than we are.

It's just good to be aware of this influence, and try to remember what WE actually think, and want, and what will actually work for our own lives.

Resentment

Resentment is one of the most toxic things in any relationship.

And one of the easiest, and most common, to feel – especially if you're the one who's been looking after the kids most.

Let's take a totally un-stereotypical family set-up, where there's a mum and a dad, and he works more while she looks after the kids more, in the Early Years.

I KNOW, I KNOW THIS IS JUST ONE WAY OF DOING IT, AND THERE ARE A GAZILLION MORE OPTIONS, OK?! I just can't write he/she you/her/him etc. to cover all possible family-structure options. Please be offended if you want to be, because YOU work while HE stays at home, or he is actually a she because you're in a same-sex couple, or a single mum, or a single dad, or neither of you work, or one of you is trans, or… fuck ME let's just take this as one example of a set-up between humans, and delete/insert/replace/wiggle about as required.

This is how it goes:

He resents you sitting at home playing with Lego.

You resent him sitting on a train listening to a podcast.

He resents your closeness with your kids.

You resent all that time alone to NOT be with kids.

He resents all that 'time off work' you're getting. (DON'T EVEN START ME.)

You resent all that time he has to work, think, play with sweet dispensers in the staff room.

He resents paying most of the bills.

You resent not being able to pay any.

He resents being stuck in a career he hates.

You resent him having one.

***

He resents you having years to think about what you'd like to do when the kids go to school, while you merrily munch on Hobnobs in toddler groups, hobnobbing with other lucky stay-at-homers, also pondering their fledgling home business making hats for refugees, while he's writing a 200-page presentation for a client who eventually doesn't pay.

You resent his having clients at all.

He resents carrying all the financial responsibility.

You resent not having a FUCKING JOB, MATE, WHICH ACTUALLY VALUES ME IN ANY WAY.

He resents being so brain-dead every evening by work stresses.

You resent not being able to USE your brain, which actually is pretty shit-hot, got me a degree and a good start in a career as a lawyer and is now rotting in a sea of *Bake Off* chat, burned oven chips and teen angst.

He resents you having all that quiet time without colleagues bitching and moaning and irritating you.

You resent having no work structure or stability and being a self-employed freelancer who's never paid and has nobody to bitch and moan to.

Etc. etc.

Resentment is ugly.

It's about perceived fairness. Jealousy. Insecurity. Self-worth.

And when we're tired, and sad about things we think we've missed out on, and envious of someone's perceived 'better, easier' life, and beaten down by looking after children who pull a sickie every Monday morning and provide never-ending school admin and sibling rivalries, we cannot perceive things fairly.

We see everything through a mist of exhaustion and 'what ifs…'

Life is never 'fair'.

It's only as fair as we decide to see it.

And we can change the way we see that, think of it, and react to it.

He has some things I don't.

I have some things he doesn't.

He had some experiences I didn't.

I had some experiences he didn't.

He worked his way up the career ladder.

I didn't. But I had more time with our kids.

I'm sure if it had been reversed, I'd have found reasons why mine was less fair.

Which is 'better'? Which is 'fair'?

I don't know. I just know that being bitter, and resenting each other, is the death of it all.

And death is quite bad.

Resentment Song

How was your day, are you feeling tired?
Did your meeting go all right? Did anyone get fired?
How was the train? Did you have to stand all the way?
Did you manage a cup of coffee – to drink in or just take away?
Poor you.
But... did I mention that I GAVE BIRTH??

Did you sort out all your documents, and answer all your calls?
Was Brian in accounting driving you up the walls?
Did you give your presentation, and manage all the... things you manage?
Did you seal the deal and leverage all of your professional advantage?
Poor you. What a DAY.
But... did I mention that I breastfed for five years, and it

fucking hurt and... LOOK AT THE STATE OF THEM NOW.

Did you pick up all the Lego, and build a hundred towers?
Did you struggle to the playground, and press a bunch of flowers?
Did you have to help with homework for the forty-seventh time?
And make a sticky picture, and sing another rhyme?
Poor you. What a DAY!
But did I mention... I'VE BEEN AT WORK ALL DAY EARNING MONEY TO PAY THE BILLS?

Did you change a load of nappies, and fold up tiny socks?
Did you pick up all the jigsaws, and put them in the box? Again.
Did you deal with hours of whining, tantrums, fighting, noise and stress?
Did you have to spend an hour persuading Millie to wear a dress?
Poor you. What a day.
But... did I mention that I've been sitting on a commuter train with my head in someone's sweaty armpit for the last two hours, unable to move or breathe?

Come here, my love.
Let me soothe your mind, and ease your day away.

Unburden all your worries, keep your stress at bay.
We're a team, you and me, supportive through and through.
But, just one little thing:
I'm WAY more tired than you.

We Are Not OWED Anything

We live in a culture of what's 'owed'. What's due to us.

What we deserve.

What we should have.

Of litigation, Rights to this, Rights to that.

It makes us angry and hateful, stressed and unhappy.

And it's not helpful – especially in a relationship.

I'm owed lots of stuff. I'm sure I owe many people lots of things too.

Counting it, trying to claw it back, get what's 'due' to me, what's fair, what's owed, is to waste what I actually HAVE, which is a life, and time to do something more positive with it, with the person I love.

I did that for a long time, after a lot of things I'd worked hard for were taken away, for no apparent reason. I was eaten up with the unfairness of it all, what I *should* have had, with counting my imbalances, with what my employers, my partner, my luck, the *world* owed me. Instead of how lucky I was to have the things I DID have, and to enjoy it.

It made me a horrible, angry person.

Instead of bringing me anything, it just wasted a lot of time and separated me from the most valuable things I had.

So I try not to do that any more. I still fail sometimes, though less often than I used to, and, when I do, I try to remember the 'life bank' thing, and that investing IN life is more rewarding than worrying about what's been taken OUT.

And then I get back to living it.

Respect

If you don't respect someone any more, you can't have a very healthy, happy relationship with them.

And it's basically over.

That's what I think, anyway.

And you can respect that opinion or not, as you choose.

Hate

Strong word; strong emotion.

It's used a lot these days.

I HATE cleaning the bathroom.

I HATE this coffee.

I HATE that bloody woman in the Post Office.

I HATE planking.

I HATE the new logo in our local coffee shop.

I HATE this weather.

I HATE YOU.

Not much point, really, hating everything.

If you really hate the person you're with, detest them, loathe them, experience intense, gut-turning dislike and hostility towards them, feel violent rage towards them and want to smash their face into the sideboard when they as much as put the toast down in the wrong way, then a) you should probably not be together right now, and b) it's almost certainly not making you hugely endearing or likeable to them either, if we're honest.

Or to anyone else.

Or to yourself.

All in all, hate is something to either let go of, or, if you really can't, then… yeah. Maybe it's not quite gonna work out.

Hate goes in the Box Of Ugly Things. Lose it.

Scar Tissue

Scar tissue is 'Fibrous matter that forms when normal tissue is destroyed by disease, injury, surgery… or long-term cohabitation.'

Scar tissue forms when a wound heals after a cut, burn or massive argument over whether it's OK for an eight-year-old to use Facebook and WHY THE HELL DID YOU LET HIM HAVE AN ACCOUNT WHEN WE'D SPECIFICALLY AGREED HE CAN'T??

Scars can also form inside the body.

And inside a relationship.

They're a permanent map of our life's knocks, bumps and pains.

Even when they fade, they're still there.

A little reminder of what caused it, what hurt, and what we don't want to repeat.

Every relationship brings its scars.

But if they keep being joined by more and more fresh ones, and if they never seem to heal properly, it might be time to work out what's causing them and to move away from it a little.

***

The thing causing the scars could be you.

It's easy to assume that our problems are caused entirely by other people, things and circumstances: a sudden wheat intolerance or early menopause or Insta-trolling from some sad, old bitch in Penzance who just seems to have it in for you, even though you only post photos of cake and coffee, and what's her fucking PROBLEM anyway?

Often, it IS all those things. Especially the bitch in Penzance.

But it's worth considering that it *might* just be caused by ourselves, too.

A lot of my shit was caused by me. Definitely.

But at the time I was too busy being all angry and resentful about my scars to notice I was actually making some of them. Maybe I was the one who had to change the way I reacted to certain things, how I behaved, and what I had BECOME as a person?

Not an easy thing to admit to oneself, that.

But one to consider – and try to learn from.

We Need to Talk… So Let's Not

I went a whole decade not talking about things we needed to talk about.

I shovelled and shovelled everything we needed to talk about under that relationship carpet until it looked like K flipping 2.

I just couldn't do it.

Maybe if I kept shovelling, it would all just… go away.

Maybe it wasn't all that important after all.

Maybe we were too knackered at the end of every parenting day to want to talk about why one of us finds it so fucking intolerable that nobody replaces the toilet roll until there are seven empty tubes balanced on top of each other like a cardboard circus act in the corner of the bathroom, and why is it MY job when I already do most of the other jobs and DON'T CITE COOKING AS A JOB BECAUSE YOU BLOODY LOVE COOKING SO IT'S HARDLY A CHORE, IS IT, MATE??!

Maybe if we leave it, it'll just… go away.

Or maybe one day the carpet will explode, as carpets do, and we will get divorced. FABULOUS WORK.

I wish I'd talked about more of it.

Early.

And calmly.

And as many times as it took.

Calmly.

And not just waited until I wanted to shove every fucking empty toilet roll tube down his throat. Not calmly.

Then at least, whatever the outcome, it would have been made in the right way, and not by face-planting over a giant carpet mound of undiscussed Lifeshit.

I Love You But I Can't Love You

Sometimes we want to love someone, but we don't.

We *should* still love that someone, because they've not really done anything obvious that would make us not still love them. But we just don't.

We want to want to grow old together, but the idea fills us with dread.

We want to make things better, but we can't.

There's no 'reason'. We just… can't.

Sometimes we don't want to make things better any more.

Sometimes we love somebody so much it hurts, but we can't love them in the way it takes to live with them forever.

Disney didn't make a whole lot of kids' films with this strapline, but maybe they should.

Marriage Counselling

Some people swear by it.

Some swear at it.

Some swear it saved their marriage.

Some swear it severed the last threads of a relationship that would have mended by itself, given a few vodkas and a shag of desperation.

Some would never try it.

Some go every year as a kind of relationship MOT.

We went three times, and then got divorced.

I'll let you read into that one as you choose.

I think it's fair to say that our relationship was pretty much over, at least in the way we'd both have liked it to be, at least three years before my trembling, ashamed fingers called Relate and booked an appointment.

But we both thought we should try it. It's what you do, right? Also, this way, if we did split up:

a) We'd have the emotional cushion of knowing that we did at least try to do something to save it.

and

b) We could pin the blame firmly on the counsellor and the airless Room of Doom.

£150 to blame someone else seemed worth it.

The whole thing was absolutely excruciating. Just turning up at the door, with what might as well have been a neon-lit, flashing Relate sign on the wall for all to see, felt like a public admission of failure. Everyone driving past, every cyclist, every bird and bacterium floating on the leaden air KNEW that the two of us had failed.

Not helping matters was the location, on a busy road in the middle of town, where literally everyone we knew was likely to be passing at any moment. I might as well Insta-story the whole thing, FFS.

***

Inside wasn't much better: the beige hallway smelled encouragingly of shame, misery, hatred and impending poverty, the untouched magazines on the coffee table had curled in despair, and I will never forget the forceful tap-tap-tapping sound of conclusive, condemning typing coming aggressively from a room out the back.

Sentences of life sentences.

'Dear Mr and Mrs X,

We are sorry that your marriage has come to an end. Enclosed is a gun, and two pairs of those paper thongs you get in beauty salons that nobody ever wears unless they're perverts. Please put them on, stand outside Topshop on a Saturday afternoon two weeks before Christmas, shout "I am a failure" 800 times and then shoot yourselves in the genitals.

Thank you for choosing to end your marriage with us.'

***

Honestly though, it was fucking awful and I'd never do it again.

Probably what I actually wanted was someone to agree with me. To vindicate everything I felt, and didn't feel; everything I had done, and wanted to do; everything I dreamed of, and all the dreams I'd given up on.

Amazingly, this isn't the job of a relationship counsellor.

They are there to be infuriatingly impartial, nonjudgemental, and to enable two people who can't be near each other, in case one of them accidentally coughs in an annoying way, to relate to each other better.

And I guess if I learned one thing from those counselling sessions, it was that we couldn't.

We couldn't relate to each other better at that time, because we couldn't actually relate to each other at ALL any more. I felt so messed up, depressed, angry, resentful, hateful, tired, frustrated, abandoned and confused, I couldn't even relate to the chair I was sinking into, let alone a man I'd made three children with.

Fuck relating better. Fuck balance. Fuck other people's opinions. I wanted a platform for MY opinions, my feelings and my points, and I wanted them to finally be heard, uninterrupted, unchallenged. Most of all I wanted someone who was definitely NOT going to agree with my partner on anything, but was going to agree with meeeeeeeeeeeee.

I wanted someone to say:

'YES!! Liz, you are right! You are brilliant! Literally everything you've said is totally BANG ON, everything you feel is totally justified, and everything you've done is totally vindicated. In a nutshell, Liz, YOU WIN!'

This is not why one should go to marriage counselling.

This is why one should go out and get pissed with some friends.

I didn't. I didn't know who to talk to.

Probably the person I needed to talk to most of all was myself.

Honestly.

And to tell myself that the truth of the matter is that your relationship, such as it was, is over, to stop being a wuss, stop lying to yourself, stop lying to him, stop lying to the world, and face it.

Realise it, acknowledge it, mourn it, and deal with it.

Then we could all move on.

I wish I'd known that.

3b: Moving Apart

According to Neil Sedaka's 1962 smasher, breaking up is hard to do (do down dooby doo, down down).

This is true. It IS hard to do. If I may, though, Neil…

Breaking up when you have kids, a mortgage, huge numbers of mutual friends, a joint bank account, a career you largely sacrificed in order to raise your children, while your partner rose steadily up the career ladder one 'drinks-with-clients-in-a-hip-hotel-in-New-York' rung at a time, shared ownership of a car (plus insurance), a dog, an Amazon Prime account and a fifteen-year-old yucca plant given to you both by a now-deceased grandmother, is very, very, very, very fucking hard to do.

In fact, it's one of the hardest things most people will ever doooooby do, down down.

***

I never intended to do it.

Amazingly enough, almost nobody *intends* to do it.

We don't get trussed up in a dress that looks like a swan has hit a landmine, cut a £350 cake that nobody wants anyway because they're too drunk by this stage to chew through the icing, make all manner of promises to each other and then trash our bodies, minds and finances to produce offspring, all the while intending to throw it away one day.

Despite the fact that we, whose marriages sadly come to an end, are still often portrayed as slap-dash, careless, selfish, and not having tried hard enough to 'make it work', most of us did try. Really hard. For years.

But eventually, we had to come to the horrible, sad conclusion that it just wasn't going to.

That trying to be happy, pretending to be happy, 'working on' being happy, buying books about being happy, creating Instagram accounts to make us look happy, desperately trying to be happy for the sake of the children, the dog, the convenience of a shared credit card, our parents, and the state of our increasingly parched under-eye skin, was just prolonging the actual, unshakable, unhappy unhappiness.

And so we did the hardest thing; we did a Neil Sedaka.

Not just a break-up, but the total, monumental, irreparable decimation of everything we had built, worked on, loved and believed in. And everything our children believed in too.

On a scale of 1–10 of hard, it's 25 billion. It pisses on three weeks of infuriating admin to get a cancelled Ryanair flight refunded, learning how to blend eye-shadow properly or trying to change your utilities provider.

It's mind-shatteringly hard.

But you can do it. And you can survive. And you can be happy again.

Millions of perfectly nice, kind, thoughtful, loving, caring, responsible, low-carbon-footprint-leaving people do it every year, and are glad, ultimately, that they did.

I just wish I'd known a few things about marriage break-up, the practical and emotional realities of it, how to deal with it, what I'd feel, what my mind and body would go through, what my children would go through, and how to re-pot a fifteen-year-old yucca plant, much, much earlier than I did.

So here is what I learned… in case it helps, consoles or amuses anyone else going through it – though I truly hope you don't.

But just as for unexpected haemorrhoids, it's best to be prepared.

The Myths of Separation

I was terrified of my marriage ending.

I've thought back many times about what it was that prevented me from letting go of the last fraying threads of a failing marriage, years after it had quite clearly unravelled beyond all repair even by the most gifted love-seamstress, and for at least five years longer than was in any way reasonably bearable, fun, sane or sensible.

What made me cling on to it by my worn old teeth like a terrier to a rotten piece of wood that's been buried in a sheep carcass for a year and stinks of decay, despair and… divorce.

What, in fact, makes any person stay in a situation which makes them unhappy, unwell, and unable to live the life they want to live, and could live if they just… dared to change?

And I think I've concluded that it's very simple, and very human.

It was FEAR.

Complete and utter terror.

I was terrified of splitting up – for all of us.

Why?

Oh, well, let's see now:

I was terrified of destitution, social castigation, maternal devastation, family rejection, lifelong regret, loss of stability, security, friends, family and our joint IKEA family card.

We'll come to all of these things in a minute, but first, here's the crux of the Terror, and the reason I shat my lady-pants at the mere thought of splitting up.

It was because the narrative I'd grown up with, of what happens when two people split up if they have children, went a bit like this:

SPLITTING UP RUINS YOUR KIDS. WHAT THE FUCK ARE YOU DOING?!

It's a subtle message, I think you'll agree, but one that screamed in my maternal DNA every miserable day and night throughout the breakdown of my relationship, holding it together with a giant Pritt-Stick of fear.

You can write any variation of it you like, watch any film, read any novel, poem, screenplay or pithy tweet about it, but the central, calming, supportive, empathetic and deeply consoling message was always the same:

Splitting up is the worst thing you can ever do to your children.

Murdering them would be kinder. Force-feed them deep-fried, chocolate-filled diabetes cookies, give them seventeen hours of screen time a day, chain them to the sofa and play them violent, misogynist rap on repeat. FUCK IT, they're fine.

Just don't, DON'T, be a SPLIT FAMILY.

Given this joy-filled message of hope and optimism, it's pretty understandable why so many people are frightened of doing something as shocking and selfish as calling time on an already-dead relationship that's suffocating the whole family.

Four years down the line and having been through it, and met countless other parents who have done the same and, amazingly, have also lived to tell the tale, have perfectly happy, functioning children and, SHOCK HORROR, have gone on to have a happy, stable and healthy new family set-up, I want to briefly rewrite the Book of Doom, tell you what I wish I'd known before we committed Family Hara-kiri, and offer a slightly more realistic, positive and supportive version of how it can be.

And almost certainly will be.

ALL THE WHAT IFS...

The 'what if's stopped me doing the actual If, for years.

I was trapped by the 'what if's. And most of them were, it turned out, wholly unnecessary.

What if... I'll regret splitting up

I think I held on to the 'what if' of regret tightest of all.

What if one day, years after the break-up carnage had all been cleared up, now happily ensconced in my new family set-up, maybe with a new partner, or no partner, a new job, a new place to live, a new set of friends, a killer New Me haircut and a new life, what if I looked back at everything that had ensued, surveyed the remains of a once-happy family that still dutifully gathered for mutual children's birthdays and graduations, at the financial fallout for us all, the photos I never dared look at any more in case it triggered a three-week weep-fest, and took out the old wedding ring I still kept in my jewellery box because it had so much sentimental value I couldn't throw it away, and also it might still be worth enough to pay the late filing penalty for my tax return.

WHAT IF I LOOKED AT ALL THIS, AND REGRETTED OUR DECISION TO END IT?

And what if I lived the rest of my life with this regret?

Well, here's the thing: I might indeed regret it.

I might also regret a whole lot of bad things that have happened, or that I've made happen, in my life. And in all likelihood, I WILL regret a lot of it.

But we can also regret *not* doing things.

Not taking a chance. Not finding something, if not better, then at least different.

Something we really felt was right, at the time.

Edith Piaf wrote a song about this. I think it was called 'Je Ne Give Pas Les Fucks'.

Edith is a good mentor for the hesitant, and her message of non-regret, of non-fuck-giving is very popular these days, where fucks are proudly not given on a huge scale.

BUT… however fabulously coiffed, sassy and full of French balls Edith was, I think her words should come with a little warning; there's a strong tendency these days, especially in the current loud, shouty, sleeves-rolled, lippy-wearing culture of

'YOU GO, GIRL! YOU GOT THIS!'

to forget that some of us DO give the fucks. All of them.

That some of us don't just flip the finger at all worries, 'grow a pair', go out for cocktails with our mates and post selfies of ourselves #livingmybestlife

For those of us with skin as thin as an invisible panty-liner and who live with the occasional, debilitating fear of absolutely everything, knowing what our 'best life' even is, is a daily struggle.

In fact, it IS the struggle.

And so the Liz Piaf version goes:

'Try not to *regrettez rien*, my friends, but if you do, *ça va*. *Ne givez pas les fucks*, if possible. And *ne regrette pas* doing what you really believe *est le* right thing, at this moment in your tired, confused *vie*.'

If you find that hard, and you sometimes fail in your Piaf-ness, that's completely normal, and OK.

If you ask me, it just shows you to be human.

And I'm big on that.

What if… I'll be seen as a failure

I worried a LOT about 'talk'.

The local bitching, gossiping, whispering, wide-eyed 'I KNOW, did you HEAR?!', proper playground cliquey miaow stuff. The real mature deal that lingers from those joyful childhood teasing 'in the gang' days, and never really leaves us even when we're old enough to be comforting our own children when they get the piss ripped out of their jeans too.

I thought my family would be seen as a failure by the chattering *Übermums* on the school-run block, all smugly enjoying their perfect, successful family lives and taking their vegan children to drama class at the weekend followed by fresh pastries and high-fives for how goddam happy and together they were.

Even though I knew plenty of other people whose marriages had FAILED and who were family FAILURES, and whose FAILED kids lived between two FAILED houses and ate FAILED Rice Krispies that'd lost all their snap, crackle *and* pop, and seemed to be not only vaguely alive and well but even not in rehab yet, thank you. I thought I'd be shunned and looked down upon for being unable to sustain a happy, strong relationship, or even a sham of a miserable one, and that it meant I was the massive FAILURE.

Even before we'd made the split official, I was sure I could hear the whispering and chattering at parents' evenings as my life was dissected and slagged off behind the crumpled teacher-appointments lists, gripped by hands still proudly wearing their tarnished wedding rings.

Dog-walkers on the common would discuss our family demise, shaking their heads at the sadness of it all 'for the children'; football coaches would give me a lingering look after my son's matches, as if to say, 'I know. I KNOW YOU HAVE FAILED.'

I thought I'd never be able to go to school concerts, sports days, second-hand uniform sales, local street parties, or even venture out to put the recycling bins outside on Tuesday nights, for fear of being seen.

Me, the FAILURE.

Me, the one who didn't have the strength to work on it, mend it, keep trying and see it all the way through to the marriage grave.

For the children.

Maybe I was shit in bed.

Maybe I was a naggy old nightmare to live with.

Maybe I smelled bad.

Maybe he'd shagged half of his company on a work trip to Dubai.

And the other half in Zurich.

Maybe my breasts just didn't do it for him any more.

Maybe, maybe, maybe.

I didn't know what they would say, but I knew they would be saying STUFF. Nasty stuff.

And I found myself retreating into a little corner of shame, fear and failure.

This is what actually happened:

When the news spread around our neighbourhood, which took about forty-eight seconds from the moment of The Phone Call, and got back to me before I'd even been to the loo and googled 'what to do when you are getting divorced' while I was weeing, the reaction was nothing as I had expected or feared.

In the months of relationship dissolution and seemingly never-ending tears that followed, the most common things people said to me were:

1. I'm really sorry to hear that, and hope you are all OK.

2. I'm here if you need a shoulder to cry on, or any help with the kids.

3. Good for you, guys. You've done what so many of us wish we could, but don't have the balls or energy to. I really hope this is a new lease of life for you all. I'm actually quite jealous!

This last response was the most surprising to me. But it came from so many people, not just close friends who knew us well but others I knew from around town who'd somehow heard about it, people on social media, cashiers in Superdrug, and even people I don't know at all.

I'd get a hand on my shoulder in the queue at the newsagent's; 'I just wanted to say I hope you're OK. It's a really brave, difficult thing, but it'll all work out fine, you'll see.'

I got emails from friends I'd not talked to or seen for years, who had somehow heard The News, opening up about their own marriage endings, how it all gets better, and how they are really happy now in a new relationship, the kids get on brilliantly with the new partner, and nobody has developed scurvy or lost any limbs.

I SO wish I'd known this was going to be the reaction, because I'd have been a lot more certain to go into this split more strongly, head still held up a LITTLE bit, knowing I would get so much support and understanding, not wall-to-wall slagging off or tut-tutting.

Oh, a note:

There were also those who quite clearly bitched and whispered and stopped saying hello as I passed them in the street. Those who would sit across a café from me, blatantly staring at me and talking in hushed, tutty tones to their tutty friends. You know those tones.

TUTTY TONES.

But you know what I learned about the starey tutters?

Fuck people like that.

Fuck 'em big time. Being a judgmental, snide little bitch is their choice, and their prerogative.

They can think what they like, say what they like, and assume what they like.

They know nothing about you, and nothing about your life.

Fuck people like that. Stick with the good'uns.

Last thing to remember is this: it never seemed to occur to me at the time, because my own world seemed so massively important and central to the entire working of the Universe, that everyone else has their own shit going on and doesn't really care all that much about other people's lives because they're kind of busy trying to keep their own afloat.

Gossip will always happen. Chatter will occur. Tuts will be tutted. Just ignore it all, and don't worry about what the Joneses might think of your life. The Joneses are probably fucking miserable anyway. So there.

What if... this is just a classic, severe case of midlife crisis

Every so often during the long, protracted, slow, slow, slow, slooooow breakdown towards break-up, I thought of this:

Maybe it's just a midlife wobble.

Maybe if I wait a little longer, it'll pass. Sort itself out.

Maybe it needs ONE LAST CHANCE.

I thought this every few weeks – for about five years.

I gave last chances to every last chance there was.

I gave it 'last, last, last and a little bit more just to be sure' chances.

I thought that maybe if we saw it through for just another month or five of super-fun shouting, sighing and teeth-clenching and sexual inactivity then we might sit down one night and accidentally watch *The Parent Trap* and suddenly realise we were actually not only perfect for each other but destined to be together forever, and we'd immediately fall in lust and love again and start humping over the toasted sandwich maker.

I held on to this thought, despite all chances having been used up so long ago I couldn't even see them any more.

But if you've not been in love for as long as you can remember, I think maybe the last chance saloon is closed.

What if... my extended family goes ape-shit

Let them.

It's *your* relationship.

It's *your* family.

It's your health.

It's your happiness.

It's your private business.

It's YOUR LIFE.

Only WE know what's right for us and what our relationship is really like behind closed doors, despite any shows of strained unity and togetherness we might be able to forcibly squeeze onto our tear-stained faces at family gatherings, aided by copious quantities of Great Uncle Jeremy's wine, or for the 'happy families' social media albums of your miserable, argument-filled holiday in Cornwall.

Only WE know the truth of our everyday, everynight lives. And the only people whose opinions and views we should be worrying about are those immediately connected to the situation itself – ourselves, our (ex) partner and our children.

I failed spectacularly at this. I was so scared of what my wider family would say if we split up and got divorced, the scathing criticism of how monumentally useless/weak/selfish/ungrateful I was, that it paralysed me into a kind of terror-lockdown for years.

Like a nervous little child worrying what my mummy would say if she found out I didn't really want my hamster any more because the truth is that I wanted a guinea pig in the first place but I screwed everything up because my best friend had a hamster and I thought if I just had one too I'd be more like her, and more liked *by* her, and NOW we have a stupid bloody expensive hamster cage in the garage, and a hamster who bites my fingers like some bitey rodent dickhead, and I've spent all my pocket money and made a massive mess in the kitchen with all the sawdust, and you're going to be really, really, really, really angry with me when I say I'm done with the sodding hamster situation, and I want to put it in a Jiffy bag and send it to Children in Need.

This fear of my family's potential upset about my own traumatic marital breakdown was ridiculous, madness and a total waste of my emotional energy and time, and entirely the product of my staggeringly low self-confidence.

But lots of perfectly grown-up grownups still worry about what their families will think about some kind of marital disaster on their part, especially if divorce is just NOT DONE in their family.

It can hamper every difficult, personal decision we're trying to make, and unnecessarily prolong something far beyond its sell-by date. Or even result in the wrong decision.

None of this helps when it comes to making decisions that are already putting us through the wringer.

What we need is help, love, understanding, unconditional support.

What a lot of us fear – or even get instead – is rejection, hostility, criticism, judgement, ridicule, sighing, tutting, head-shaking, family bitching over a cup of Tetley's and a custard cream, and a general total inability to accept an outcome they can't get their heads around.

I wish I'd had someone near me at the time to counsel me better, and give me the strength in myself to keep remembering these things:

This is YOUR life. Not your mother's, your aunt's or your second-cousin-once-removed's.

If there are people in your family who disapprove of the sad things that have happened to you, or are so blinkered and self-centred they can't get their heads around it or accept it yet, that's on them, not on you.

They might eventually come round.

It can take years, but in general, they do.

If they don't... so be it. That's their perspective, and their choice.

It's worth remembering that if families are critical of a split, and seem unkind or unsupportive, it's often genuinely out of kind concern for us, and a worry that we're making the wrong decision. So while it can hurt SO much to be receiving any kind of doubt or head-shaking at all, when all you need is some frickin' SUPPORT AROUND HERE PLEASE, GUYS! it might be coming from a place of love – however unhelpful to you their particular method of love-giving might be.

That said, family criticism is sometimes nothing more than pure, mean selfishness. A kind of 'your pain has just ruined MY life'.

Your ugly, stinking divorce, your embarrassing failure as a child, doesn't fit into THEIR pretty, socially peachy life plan or dream for you, or for their lovely, perfect, divorce-free family.

The deep social shame they feel, caused by YOU, is being projected back onto you, for doing this 'to them'.

Poor, poor them.

My heart bleeds. It also implores me to tell you to ignore it.

Your decision is none of their self-motivated business.

When you're cruising through your seventies, happy, fulfilled and sexually gratified by someone who loves you, you'll be glad you made the changes that were right for YOU, way back then, and ignored the family head-shaking.

Most of them probably wish they'd done the same thing thirty years ago, and had run off to live with Eduardo in Brazil. You're doing what they didn't have the kahunas to do, and they are just jealous. Maybe. Or maybe… oh who gives a fuck!

This is your life, and you have the rest of it to live. You deserve to be happy. Just keep remembering that.

What if... this is a terrible thing to do

If it's the right thing to do, it's not a terrible thing to do.

It's the right thing. (#logic)

When I was at school the number of children in my class whose parents were divorced was… zero.

Literally none.

In that class of twenty-one, the number of children whose parents were quite visibly miserable, frustrated, sad, lonely and allergic to each other was at least nineteen and a half, on a good day.

But splitting up was just not done.

You sort of soldiered on, however devastatingly unhappy your drooping face suggested you were, gritting your worn teeth and smiling on cue at the school concert before numbing your sorrows in gallons of free prosecco and telling yourself it's all OK because staying together was The Right Thing To Do.

And always, the people it was the 'right' thing for was THE KIDS.

We were possibly the last generation of children (and now parents ourselves) who were raised to fear and believe that divorce is the Devil's rotting cyst.

The ultimate act of selfish, cruel, reckless, narcissistic, thoughtless self-obsession. A failure. A disaster.

Thankfully, we are now a little more understanding of the fact that sometimes relationships just don't work out. That families exist in all different forms, not just 2.4 children and grim determination. And that staying together FOR THE KIDS isn't the right reason.

On which note…

What if… my kids will be fucked up

Welllll, they might be.

But this not being the year 1923, and us not being completely unaware of how hard splitting up can be on children, in all likelihood they will not be fucked up.

I didn't believe this for a long time. Etched deep into my parenting bones was the ancient, blood-chilling warning that:

Splitting up RUINS YOUR CHILDREN.

Destroys their entire life, and leads to failure at school, social problems, substance abuse and poor taste in music.

This outcome causes a lot of parents to sit in abject misery for decades, simply to avoid it.

'Broken families lead to broken children, Elizabeth!' I was told.

I was actually told this! By someone with a frickin' PhD.

A PhD in what, exactly – complete disconnection from reality?

'Broken families', as no reasonable, intelligent person calls them any more, do not lead to broken children.

Miserable families might.

Families full of anger and fighting might.

Families with thirty years of unresolved conflict might.

Families radiating hate and violence might.

But families where mummy and daddy don't live together any more, don't.

Children nowadays have grown up in a very different 'norm' anyway, and it's very likely that loads of their mates have parents who are no longer together, or possibly never even were, and now have new partners, half-siblings, step this-and-that, and are very happy, thank you.

I wish I'd known this before our family went through 'the change', and I went through my break-up, breakdown and break flipping everything. My children saw me crying almost every day, visibly exhausted, stressed, losing so much weight they could play the xylophone on my ribs, and I was not being in any way the strong, coping mum they needed then. I was so traumatised by the split, by the fallout, by the fear of what it would do to them all, by depression and self-loathing, that I barely coped with anything at all.

If I'd just been given the assurance and confidence to believe that whatever shape our family had now, showing my children that mummy was OK, and in this new, happy, strong state could be a better mummy for THEM and make THEM happier, it could have been a lot easier all round.

What if... I'll be destitute

I'm not sure how to break this to you gently, so I'll just smack you over the head with it and see how you get on.

You will be destitute.

OK, not destitute, maybe, but the ugly, skint truth of splitting up is that very few people end up financially better off for it. Dividing all your assets in half and chucking a summer holiday in Tuscany's worth of that at a lawyer, is hardly a top business plan, if we're honest.

You know those people you read about who go from divorce to divorce cleaning up their exes' millions, living in ever-bigger houses, going on holiday six times a year and killing it on the glowing-skin front?

Yeah, well that's bollocks for the rest of us, my friend.

Think less 'gold-digger', and more… 'loose-change-scrabbler'.

The painful fact is that, in financial terms, splitting up – and even more so, divorcing – fucks us up the backside with a sizzling hot poker. And not in a good way.

Because amazingly enough, life is a little easier with two incomes than with one.

It's a weird kind of 'up yours' maths that says:

1 income + 1 income = 2 incomes, all fine and dandy, off we go to B&Q to buy a new lawnmower and some bedding plants. It's OK, because we CAN AFFORD IT.

BUT

What no maths teacher ever told you is that, in family economics terms, 1 on its own is not half of 2.

It's about... minus twenty-five grand.

Before tax.

Even if you're a one-income family to begin with, it's STILL easier when you live together and share this one income.

If you're getting off on the maths thing, then that's sort of:

1 + 0 = 12 + work perks.

Why? OK, let's see now.

First of all, when you're together you live in the same house.

Minor detail.

As a result, you pay one set of utilities bills, have one shared Netflix account, one shared home insurance, one shared council tax bill, one shared lot of costs for building work, boiler-fixing and so on.

When you split, you are very likely to have to start living in separate places, unless you have a verrrrrrry unusual set-up where you hate each other but still share a roof.

I know quite a lot of couples who did this for a while – for the kids, for the trembling bank balance, to avoid telling his mum who has a heart problem – but eventually realised they wanted to disembowel their ex-husband or wife with one of the fondue forks they were given when they got married and have never used.

But for most people, it's like the Spice Girls in reverse, and one becomes two.

Amazingly, two properties cost more than one.

It's just like Monopoly, but without the cute little top hat and iron.

Moving on down

When one house is divided into two, they are generally much smaller than the original one. Smaller, and often further away from school, from work, and with less space for all the kids' things.

Downsizing at a time when you expected to be doing the opposite can feel like a kick in the teeth, when most of your teeth were already starting to fall apart.

Of course anyone is lucky if they can afford to live in a house at ALL, but it doesn't mean that taking a giant knock down the property-comfort ladder, from something large enough for you all, with a garden for the paddling pool and a basketball hoop, to a place so small you have to sell your son's entire Lego collection and throw away most of your children's non-essential toys, clothes and books just to be able to open the front door, doesn't feel so good.

Bills

The costs of living separately can mount up as blood-chillingly fast as the bank balance goes down.

From home insurance and general house maintenance to council tax, Wi-Fi, gym membership, car insurance and subscriptions to iTunes, Netflix and every goddam thing Adobe makes – you're now BOTH paying this instead of sharing it.

And THEN… there are school uniforms and PE kits, music classes, ballet exams, cinema trips (HOW MUCH IS A CINEMA TICKET THESE DAYS??!!), new trainers for your teenagers' ludicrously giant feet, scientific calculators for their GCSEs, gizmos and whatnots you can't afford but they claim they NEED in order to survive socially/academically/emotionally/anally, new headphones because they sat on their old pair, reading glasses and, let's not even mention… SCHOOL TRIPS.

School trips = enforced destitution or lifelong guilt-trip.

Honestly though, do they HAVE to go all the way to Norfolk in a stinking coach to measure offshore drift? For thirty-five quid? Plus the obligatory fish'n'chips for a further tenner. Really??! Could they not just… YouTube it or something?

And that's before we even start to talk about such household extravagances as food, drink, toilet paper and Maoams.

Replacing all the stuff

'Stuff' is hard to quantify, and largely depends on your split circumstances. Some people divide everything. Others kick one party out, and that person has to pretty much set up home again from scratch.

I was in such shock after we split up that I gave absolutely everything we jointly owned to him and my kids, and moved into a house down the road that contained… almost nothing.

And in terms of stuff, it had, like… zilch. Not even a plug for the kitchen sink. It was fully, certifiably, terrifyingly stuff-free.

And I hadn't realised until then just how much shit we all have in our lives just to survive the perilous journey from getting up to going to bed.

Or how much it all COSTS to replace.

The last time I'd set up home I was also getting married, and we were handily and kindly given everything we needed by our friends and family. (Including an impressive seven salad bowls. Was there a global salad bowl rush in 1996?! We will never know how this happened, but they came in very useful when our teenagers started having house parties and needed containers for their highly questionable cocktails.)

Anyway. I needed new EVERYTHING.

New cutlery – WHY IS CUTLERY SO EXPENSIVE when it's just heat-proof fingers? – new crockery, new frying pans, new pots, a new colander, new bowls (anyone got a spare salad bowl, perchance? I used to have seven…), a draining board, a microwave, scouring pads, a sieve, a hand mixer, wooden spoons, tea towels, bath mat, toilet brush, towels, bedding, light, spare bulbs, scissors, Sellotape, kettle, pillow cases, sheets, a pedal bin, a tool kit, bedside lights… MY GOD the list of things we have in our homes that we didn't realise we had until we need to REPLACE THE WHOLE GODDAM LOT!

So off to IKEA I went, like a good soon-to-be-divorcee, and just got the whole bang-shoot. Over a grand's worth of replacement STUFF.

My bank account had a small heart attack.

Now, all of this is pretty obvious, and you're a smart human so you know splitting up is going to be hard on the wallet.

It's part and parcel of the whole Split Hoopla, and if we're happier in the long run to be out of a broken, abusive, sad or just run-out relationship, then it's a pay-off (most unfortunate choice of expression ever) we are prepared to take.

But the extent of my financial fuckery after splitting up was something I was totally unprepared for, and it hit me harder, in more unexpected, emotional ways, than I could have imagined.

It had a hugely negative and deeply damaging effect on my mental and emotional wellbeing, and I wish I'd known much more about this right at the start, and had put some things in place to deal with it better.

I might also have taken a few more salad bowls. And maybe the microwave. And the car.

What if... I never find love again

This isn't a worry for now.

This is about your relationship NOW, the one that you're actually in, and are struggling with.

It's about whether the relationship you're in NOW is right for you, your partner, your kids, and your lives going forward.

It's not about any potential/maybe/possible/future relationships that may or may not happen.

Worrying about never finding the right person isn't a reason to stay with the wrong one.

And yeah. You'll find love again, if you want it.

You really will.

What Kind of Mother Are You?!

Splitting up when you have kids is generally pretty horrendous for all concerned. (Except the lawyers, and whichever one of you gets to keep the AeroPress.)

It's hard, not only on the children, obviously, but also – and we mustn't forget this in all the concern over those children – really hard on their parents.

However it all pans out in the end, immediately after a break-up there is so much pain to live with it's hard to carry it about in your giant under-eye bags, and, for parents, two of the heaviest are these:

You almost certainly won't be living with your children every day any more, and:

You also have the searing pain of knowing every minute of every day that you've just put them through a traumatic experience they never asked for, don't deserve, and would have been better without.

Now, it's hard on both parents (assuming both of them

actually WANT to be with their kids, and care about them – which, sadly, isn't always the case).

But I'm gonna say one thing about this, and I'm prepared to be damned and hated for all eternity if it upsets anyone out there with a penis:

I think it's harder for mums.

There. I said it. * Takes cover *

I don't say this because I'm a shouty, bra-waving, ball-breaking man-hater. I say it because it's just GENERALLY harder for mums. I don't even say it for the obvious reasons that we grew them, carried them inside us for months, gave birth to them, nurtured them, and were physically and emotionally attached to them for a huge chunk of their early lives, causing a deep connection of the psyche that's almost unbearable to pull apart.

This is true, of course, and it's a huge factor.

But another reason, often unspoken but carried on the strong current of Maternal Rules, is this:

Mothers don't leave their young.

Even if said young now have acne and braces, are taller than us, smarter than us, stronger than us, doing their GCSEs and trying at every opportunity to mate with the spot-infested offspring of the cave next door, they are still, technically, our young.

Other species have it far easier; they kick their young out of the nest to go fend for themselves and set up home in another tree/burrow/cave within days of their first solid poo.

Some even eat their babies, which, even after a particularly brain-smashing run of sleepless nights and teenage strops, seems a little harsh to me.

But for humans it's different. Human mummy lion doesn't abandon her baby lions.

Ever.

There's no 'Get Out Of Parenting Responsibilities' card, which sweeps the guilt, blame, shame, failure and social castigation under a giant Mumcarpet.

For a woman, a MOTHER, to be the one to say:

'I can't do this any more. I am going to smash up my children's whole understanding of family life, love, trust and safety, and throw them out into the freezing wasteland of Broken Families to meet their fate in the hands of the school's counselling service and Insta stories about self-harm.

'I'm going to do the one thing I've been told I mustn't do, as a mother.

'And I'm doing it for… me. Because I'm so unhappy in this relationship that I'm going to be selfish, cruel and devoid of all maternal instinct to nurture and protect my vulnerable, precious young, currently upstairs perfectly happily watching *Brooklyn Nine-Nine*, eating Wotsits and FaceTiming people they don't know, and leave their father.'

To even think about it means we should have our ovaries ripped out and their skins (do ovaries have skins? Some kind of egg shell? Google it, I'm busy) made into mini piñatas and strung up at our child's next birthday party for them and their mates to smash to pieces with a stick made out of all the Mother's Day cards they'd foolishly drawn for their BITCH-WHORE-COW-MUM.

KILL. ME. NOW.

I asked a lot of other mums who had also gone through The Split if they felt this way, and got a highly inconclusive 100 per cent response rate of:

OH. FUCK. YES.

I'm not saying it's not hard for dads. I'm not saying they don't also experience guilt, shame, a sense of failure and immense sadness.

But for all the mums out there who feel it's just... different when you're the one with the aching womb, and that it carries more social, emotional, 'natural' and maternally shameful weight to split up and not live with your kids full time, then just know that you are not the only one who feels it.

My only small piece of advice, such as it is, would be to try and remember that this feeling of I AM THE WORST MOTHER IN THE WORLD is largely the result of social conditioning and the oft-depicted 'ideal' of motherhood that we've been raised to understand, expect and almost demand.

Both in others, and in ourselves.

In other cultures, this wouldn't even be an issue.

And there are MANY, MANY absolutely fucking fabulous, amazing, brilliant, loving, kind, supportive, strong mothers who don't live with their children seven days a week, who are not criticised or socially crucified for it, and whose kids are absolutely fine, happy and healthy, and adore their mum just as much as they did before the split happened, thank you very much.

There are many ways to be a mother.

There are many ways to be a FANTASTIC mother.

And not all of them require your presence 24/7.

This might not have been your Plan A for motherhood, but if it's the path life has chosen for you, you will make it work.

And anyone who wants to criticise you for it, can go right ahead.

You just carry on doing your best, and knowing that's good enough.

New Family Benefits

NEW SIBLINGS CAN BRING NEW HAPPINESS TO YOUR CHILDREN

I now have a daughter who's fifteen years younger than my next-youngest child. Biologically, she's their 'half' sister, but we've never called her that. She is their SISTER. And both halves of her beautiful whole have made her siblings enormously happy. They adore her, she adores them, and it's been one of the most positive things to happen to our family.

She's also made them, in their teenage years, see a side of me they would never otherwise have known: me, as a mum of a baby and toddler.

Me, as I was WITH THEM.

Happy, caring, tired, patient, working tirelessly to feed her, clean her, play with her, educate her, show her the world, wipe her nose/bum/face/hands/knees, and generally MOTHER THE CRAP OUT OF HER.

Exactly as I did for them.

I think it's made them far more appreciative of how hard it was raising the three of them, and how much I absolutely loved looking after them. Taking them to toddler groups. Making gingerbread men. Finger-painting. Reading stories over and over and over and over again. Rocking them to sleep. Crying in the bathroom when they wouldn't go to sleep.

And that they should maybe cut me some frickin' SLACK for the several hundred fuckups I made along the way.

I did my best. And it was pretty OK.

A NEW PARTNER CAN BE BRILLIANT FOR YOUR KIDS

Ah, the Evil Stepmother of fairy-tale fame. The 'vile new boyfriend' our children love to hate.

Yes, this can happen. Especially if your new partner is, in fact, evil or vile or any other variation of those letters. But they can also be hugely liked and welcomed by your kids.

Awesome Thing 1: is that they are not your children's parent. As such they don't carry any of our parental annoyances, irritations and eye-rolling potential.

Awesome Thing 2: is that they can see things from a new perspective, that's not clouded by years of arguing and memories of That Shit Weekend in Norfolk, or financial unfairnesses. They can be neutral, balanced and detached from all that. And for kids, this can be a huge relief.

Awesome Thing 3: a new partner can be a great new confidante, and source of support, care and Haribos. Also, an invaluable channel for your kids' feelings about YOU.

My children told my new partner all the personal shit about me they felt they couldn't say to me. He could listen, be completely nonjudgemental, and, crucially, he didn't tell me. This confidence meant they could get a whole lot of things off their heavy chests, and have a good bitching session about me.

If that's an evil stepdad, then I'll take two, please.

My Baby Counsellor

Stop.

Our children are not our counsellors, nor should they feel they need to be a source of sympathy or support for us. That's *our* job, for *them*.

When my marriage ended, I think a part of me wanted my children to see that I was really struggling with it all, too, and I wasn't just dancing off into a new, happier life of parties, spa breaks and freedom.

In some selfish, needy, guilt-fuelled way, I was trying to gain some kind of sympathy or forgiveness from the very people who had been hurt through no fault of their own, by looking as sad, broken and hurt as possible.

This is bullshit behaviour, and I wish I'd employed the, 'children are happy if mummy is happy' thing, and shown them that I'm OK, so they are going to be OK, and I'm here for *them*.

I didn't. I was a wreck. And I'm sure it had a negative impact on them for a while.

I feel really bad about this, but we all feel bad about some of the shitty parenting stuff we've done.

We've done it, there's no undoing it, and we can only say our sorries, give them a hug/giant Byron burger with extra fries AND milkshake, and move on.

And try not to do it again.

One Shit Doesn't Fit All

Everyone is different.

Everyone's life is different.

And everyone's shit is different.

Your shit is your shit. And only you know how YOU feel about that.

Someone else might look at your shit from outside and say:

'Dude, your shit is OK! My shit is WAY worse than yours.'

And you'd be looking at their shit, thinking the exact same.

Everyone is just out there, looking at each other's shit from afar, with no idea what it's actually composed of, how bad it smells, or how long it's been lying there covered in flies.

It doesn't matter what other people think.

All we can do is know our own shit, try to clear it up as much as we can, but if it's still there, smeared across our Lifepavement making our souls stink, then it's time to move away from it.

And that, my friend, is maybe the biggest pile of steaming relationshit, you'll ever read.

But I believe it. Take it, and use in whatever way it works for YOU.

Please just wipe carefully, and flush.

Divorce Isn't An Ugly Word

It's not really all that surprising that we think of divorce as a putrid blot on our otherwise rosy landscape, when almost everything about the way we talk about it and deal with it is so staggeringly negative.

Even the vocabulary we use for splitting up, and for the new-look family set-up it leaves us with, is a giant finger-flip to the spirit of all hope, positivity and moving forward to better things:

Divorced parents – where the word 'divorce' derives from the Latin 'catastrophus selfishus monumentalus'.

Split families.

Broken homes.

Half-siblings, as if it's not possible to be anything whole any more.

Stepmum – that well-known literary figure of love, kindness and maternal warmth who generally kidnaps, murders, eats or psychologically tortures her new partner's children until they run away into the woods and are finished off by werewolves.

Just filling in a simple gym membership form can leave even the most resilient of us feeling like a social cast-off and child-wrecker.

Name:

Address:

Relationship status. Please delete as appropriate: married, happily single, happily dating, SELFISHLY DIVORCED.

It shocked me how many examples I came across in everyday life, from newspapers to films, to just overheard in the queue at Tesco, that made a parental split sound almost worse than infanticide.

This, in a world where so many perfectly kind, thoughtful, demonstrably un-monstrous people I knew either had split up already or were going through it (or clearly should be going through it) and whose families actually seemed better for it.

Why did these people still have to hear the terms 'broken home', 'split family' and so on, used about them? How was this in any way representative of the new, better situation they found themselves in, or supposed to support or encourage any of them in the difficult, upsetting and exhausting process they were crawling their way through?

It's cruel, unkind and deeply unhelpful.

Luckily, new terms are emerging:

Blended family, new family or just… MY FRICKIN'

FAMILY, OK?! are all a tad more positive than 'split' or 'broken'.

And the sooner they stop asking us to tick 'divorced/separated' on forms, as if it's some kind of statement about our suitability to rent a car for the weekend, the better all round.

We're not 'split' families.

We're not 'broken'.

We're reshaped, changed, blended, brave, strong, supportive, liberated, reborn, unified, together and just… new.

We are new families. Like a jelly, melted down again and poured into a new mould.

We are new jellies, wobbling about in new ways.

And many of them are very welcome additions to the family table.

Yes, You Are Allowed to Divorce a Nice Guy

As if everything in my midlife meltdown wasn't stressful enough already, my ex just had to go and be a REALLY NICE GUY.

The bastard.

By being such a goddam NICE GUY he fucked everything up for me, in terms of citing any reasonable grounds for us to split up.

As far as I'd understood it, the only acceptable reasons for putting all your belongings into cardboard boxes and throwing most of your kids' inheritance down the drain, were big-ass things like abuse, lying, cheating, gambling, being a shit parent, being a shit partner, being in any other way some obviously, visibly, demonstrably shit kind of person.

My ex-husband is a decent, kind, supportive, stable, honest, reliable, handsome, fit man. And a good dad.

Fucksake.

But there was ONE problem I could confidently point my ring-weary finger at, and shout to anyone who asked why the hell we were splitting up:

We didn't want to be together any more.

That was it. And that was enough.

We were no longer who we had been, when we disappeared into the long, exhausting, nappy-laden Parenting Tunnel all those years ago. We just weren't the same PEOPLE. Individually, or as a couple.

And we weren't in love any more.

Try as we might to flog the dying horse of love (you read that Greek myth, right?), find a new way to be together, to be in love, to be happy, and to be greater together than the sum of our two sadly drooping parts, the truth was that together, we added up to:

Fuckyouirritatemesomuch x 4795.

We went to the counselling, did the talking, the shouting, the long silences, the crying, the experimenting with various things, and the soul-searching (key here is to have a soul you actually want to search, and I'm not sure I did any more by that stage; mine was shrivelled and angry, resentful and sad, and should've been left well alone to simmer in its own misery until it felt better), we just weren't… living any more.

We were existing at best, and slowly decomposing at worst.

And strangely enough, a slow, rancid, painful decomposition just wasn't quite what we wanted for the next forty years.

So THAT needs to be added to the list above. However nice he may be, however useful with sorting out your tax return, however sweet you find his mum's little touches for the kids' stockings at Christmas, however much you like the shape of his neck, however many good memories you have together from way back when you still made each other laugh, however many good things there might still be, it's still possible that on some level that's vital to YOU to be happy in your life:

It

Just

Isn't

Working

Any

More

And that's OK.

You don't need to justify your decision to anybody, explain it, reason it or have a single person in the world agree with it.

It's YOUR decision. And only you need to know why.

What's Getting Divorced Actually Like?

Divorce – or any separation after many years together – where children are involved, is one of those things you can't really imagine until you get one. ('Get one'? That makes it sound like a dishwasher or a hernia. It feels considerably more like the latter.) Point is, you won't know how it will affect you until you do it.

And everyone's is different.

A bit like orgasms.

But actually more like… a disembowelling. Of your entire SOUL.

Divorce, even when you want it, it's the right thing to do and everyone will definitely be better off for it in the long run, is generally awful. Really, really awful.

It's hard to describe just how awful, and in how many varied ways of awful, because almost nothing you will ever have encountered before comprehensively covers All Things That

Are Awful quite as much as splitting up with someone you once loved, and with whom you have shared holidays and friends' weddings and shower gel and nail clippers and bodily fluids and children.

So. Here are some things I learned about divorce, that nobody told me before it happened:

DIVORCE MADE ME VILE

One of the worst things about splitting up, for me, was what it did to me as a person – and how VILE it made me.

Horrible, awful, ghastly, ugly vile. The worst kind of vile.

I became filled with almost nothing but hatred, rage, embitterment, more hatred, regret, bitterness, rage, envy, sadness, (did I mention rage?), despair, loathing, terror and spite, which quickly translated back into rage.

All in all, I wasn't the loveliest person in the world to be around, and all of this negativity and anger did immense damage to my mental and physical health, hair thickness and skin tone. And it wasn't the best for those around me either.

Almost everyone I've ever known who's gone through a family break-up with kids, even if they came out of it pretty well, has experienced something similar. And, most often, the person who feels the most rage and hatred is to be the one who feels they did the most to raise those children. Who 'gave' the most. Who sacrificed the most. Who, in their mind, is somehow owed the most in return. And who is thus raging the most.

They might not be right, but they feel it.

If you find yourself expressing any of the following loving sentiments, possibly through gritted teeth and while wielding a cast-iron griddle about your head, you are quite normal:

'I gave up my whole career to raise your children! You're only sitting pretty at the top of your frickin' career ladder because I stayed at the bottom, wiping your children's noses for a decade, and propping it up for you. I hate you.'

'Just LOOK at the state of my body after I sacrificed it for our children – you think anyone will want to shag THIS now? Really? Fuck you, with your stretch-mark-free body. I hate you.'

'You're a man – you can have kids until you're ninety-five. My child-bearing days are OVER. I'm done. Spent. Pointless. A hollow echo chamber of resentment. I'll put that on my Tinder profile, shall I? I HATE YOU.'

'Your earning potential is approximately 10 billion times higher than mine, you jammy piece of knob-wank, because amazingly enough it's a tad hard to crawl back into a highly paid job when you haven't attended a work meeting for five years, still have to do the school run, look after them when they're ill, help to fill in their UCAS forms, and be available 24/7 to deal with teenage heartache and hair problems. I HATE YOU!'

'I hate you.'

'I fucking HATE YOU for everything you have, and I don't.'

'Fuck you.'

'Fuck fuck fuck fucking fuck everything about you.'

'And no, you can't keep the books. I CHOSE ALL THE BOOKS. They are my books. (Except the ones about how to be an effective manager. You can have those. I hope you die reading them.)'

This was the kind of calming internal – and occasionally loud, external – rhetoric I experienced just after we split up.

It was constant, incessant, every day and night, for months.

I stewed and boiled in a level of hatred I've never known. A rage I'd never experienced before, except once in Sainsbury's when the woman in front of me started to count out £12.74 in loose change, and I was already twelve minutes late for ballet pick-up time.

It was a rage that felt genuinely terrifying, for its sheer magnitude:

I wanted to rip, cut, hit, slash, tear, smash and hurt. Everything.

Every day.

I would wake up in the night, my bed soaked in sweat, fists clenched, teeth clenched, whole body clenched, even my brain clenched if it could do it, having woken from another exhausting dream where I was attempting to smash my ex's face to pieces with my knuckles but couldn't because he was laughing at me from behind a six-foot poster at a conference, which everyone was loving.

Enraged but pathetic, futile, ineffective, powerless, humiliating thrashing about and arm-wielding.

All this negativity was totally pointless.

It did nothing but destroy things. Damage, hurt and break them.

It exhausted me, and gained me nothing.

And for our children, it was a shining example of how not to behave in a mature, calm, rational way.

After much passing of time and gin, I decided a slightly better way to proceed was to put all the hatred and resentment aside into a mental box, close it, recognise that there was fault on both sides, and try to see the GOOD things about my life going forward.

And try – TRY – not to hate someone I had once loved.

It took a long time. I opened the box many times and hated, ranted, screamed and tried all that arm-flailing stuff again.

But it did, slowly, start to ease.

The Divorce System Is Designed to Make You Hate Each Other

In order to be granted the great honour of a divorce, you are pretty much legally required to PROVE how much you detest each other.

How much you have hurt, damaged and made each other unhappy beyond all repair. You have to demonstrate beyond all doubt that you cannot possibly continue living together without killing each other using hoover attachments and a blowtorch, and thus fulfil the required criteria to be given the permission to live apart, and be happier that way.

It's as if it was set up by some ancient society of guilt-mongers, who get a pay-out for every miserable marriage they save.

There STILL isn't a box to tick that says, 'Look, we are both reasonably sane, kind, intelligent individuals, we love our kids, and we are in total agreement that splitting up is best for us all. We just don't want to live together any more because, frankly, it's not been going so well for the last… FUCKINGAGES, and we'd just like to be able to say our goodbyes in a civilised way, divide our possessions equally, and go and shag the first person we meet – because we BOTH WANT THAT.'

Instead, it's one massive slag-a-thon. It's awful. And it creates far more hate than is necessary, fair or healthy.

Wait the Two Years

At the time of writing this, it's possible to have a 'no-fault' divorce after two years of separation.

'No-fault' actually means 'fault on both sides'. And there is, almost always, fault on BOTH sides.

We filled out the applications for a divorce pretty quickly after we separated, probably because we were in such emotional turmoil we needed something to focus on, and filling in sad little boxes seemed like a nice distraction from crying.

But then we both looked at the bit where one of us had had to write down all the reasons this split was the other person's fault.

And it HURT – both of us.

It was a huge, ugly, blistering, painful, forced misrepresentation of years of happy togetherness, which had come to a slow, messy, awful end.

So we ripped it up, waited another year, and filled it in again.

'No-fault.' Just... 'the way it panned out'. And that's the truth.

Play Nicely

Emotional upset can make us do things we might not otherwise do.

And divorce is one muthafucka of an emotional upset.

The temptation to seek revenge on a partner who we feel has hurt us, cause hurt to them, grab and grasp every last tiny possession we can possibly get our angry, hate-filled, tear-stained hands on, can cause far more hurt and destruction not only to ourselves, but also to our kids, than it's ever worth.

I was given the following helpful piece of advice by a friend, just at the point of my split, when I was raw and angry and frightened.

Still in his early thirties, he had already lost both of his parents, all of his inheritance, and most of everything he cared about. Several times.

But he had what he needed to live, he had friends, he had a job, and despite having been dealt more shit cards already than most of us get in a lifetime, he was pretty OK with his lot.

What, he asked me, is the point of fighting over every item you owned, every book, every piece of furniture, every penny, every kitchen utensil and every bathroom towel? Of arguing over every minute you're now allowed with your kids, who decides on their birthday theme and what they get in their packed lunch?

Do you want to live with this person? No.

So, you already have what you want. Arguing and fighting over anything just costs time, energy and money.

Let it go.

Be happy about what you DO have, and just leave the rest.

And that's what I did.

I lost a lot of money through it, I gave away a lot of things I had once loved, made, was given, and could have argued over.

But now, years down the line, I'm glad I didn't throw most of my kids' inheritance at lawyers, and just learned to LET GO.

Life moves on.

And you can always get new bathroom towels. It's really OK.

Seeing a Family Lawyer: Part 1

Why see a family lawyer? Because they've seen it all a thousand times before and know a SHIT-TON of helpful stuff about what you're going through.

That's why they are family lawyers.

Not only is a lot of this stuff useful, I also found it hugely SUPPORTIVE.

I didn't know my Rights as a mother. I didn't know what I could and couldn't ask for. (In the end I asked for nothing, but it was at least reassuring to know that I COULD if I chose to. That I existed, and there was something out there that might help me if I needed it.)

I didn't even know that my children could have a say in some of it all.

I knew nothing. And knowing nothing is to leave yourself horribly vulnerable, at an already horribly vulnerable time.

Go see a lawyer. The first appointment is sometimes free – but not always.

Check.

Seeing a Family Lawyer: Part 2

Despite all this usefulness and helpful information I got when I was there, I found going to see a family lawyer for the first time immensely distressing.

Just googling 'local family law firms' made me cry.

Going IN there was almost more than I could manage.

The last time I'd been to a lawyer it was to buy our house.

This time it was to find out if I'd even have a house by the end of the week.

The surreal-ness of this visit became more acute the closer I got to the front door.

How could this be happening to *me*?! I gargle every night after flossing, I've read the whole of *Harry Potter* to my son three times, I do my pelvic-floor exercises while I'm washing up and I separate the darks from the whites.

I don't go to DIVORCE LAWYERS.

Yet there I was. Standing in the rain outside the Door of Doom.

Entering the building felt like jumping off the end of the Plank of Life.

Grimy, finger-marked walls painted in Farrow and Ball's 'Despair' were lined from floor to ceiling with cardboard boxes, all labelled with names of the failed and fallen.

I sat on a plastic chair with a crack in it just where that really sensitive bit of skin is at the top of your thighs, filling in Forms of Disaster, in a corridor that stank of sad endings with uplifting top-notes of sadness, regret, shame and hatred.

In her office at the end of this tunnel of despair, the grim reaper of love, swishing her Law Books about, was preparing to carve up the carcass of my marriage.

Dusty windows, dusty plants, dusty business and a dusty shredder, waiting to chop our lives, our hopes, our children, our souls.

When I finally went into her office, it was like sidling in to see all the Head Teachers and Angry Bosses of the World, rolled into one.

It was brutal.

I wanted a hug.

I got a cold shower of facts.

And… of course I did. The Law doesn't care about our feelings. It only cares about the Law.

And lawyers, who are not emotionally involved, can be purely logical and factual – something I found really tough, because I was SO emotionally involved I could barely see.

Lawyers are not interested in how you feel about your

soon-to-be-ex-father-in-law, who regularly plied your kids with chocolate every time he saw them, even though you'd specifically asked him not to every time.

They don't care.

They are not there to care.

If they cared about every client's personal life they'd have a breakdown by the end of the week. They are there to tell us lots of things we didn't know, and which could really help us.

So, bring tissues. Get the info you're there to get.

Then go to the pub and cry with someone who does care. And doesn't cost £400 for the service.

Time Heals

When things are bad, Time does some weird shit.

Mainly, it SLOOWWWWWWSSSS RIIIIGHT DOOWWWNNNN.

Every day feels like an impossibly long, heavy, slow eternity (those are the WORST kinds of eternity) and just getting through one hour of one day of one interminable week can seem impossible.

If you've never been in this situation, I can't explain how hard it is to survive from 10.40 a.m. to 10.41 a.m.

It takes HUGE effort just to exist in this Time-treacle.

The slowing is especially cruel at this time, because when everything hurts so much it feels as if the air is made of razors and gravity has just tripled, crushing your lungs, brain and soul, pushing you further and further into the break-up awfulness, social fallout, financial terror and parenting guilt-warp, it would be super-convenient of Time if it hurried the fuck up and moved along as fast as it could, so things could get better.

NOW.

But they don't. They go on and on and on, and at times I remember feeling that they will NEVER get better.

Ever, ever, ever.

I believed that my new state of Total Awfulness was how it would be forever from now on, and nothing would ever be OK again.

How could it? How could anything ever go back to being OK when it was THIS BAD?

When would it be safe to go back into the world, a Divorced Woman who no longer lives with her children every day, and not be pelted by rotten shame-tomatoes?

When would my children forgive me?

When would I have any financial security again?

When would I feel HAPPY again?

Would I EVER feel happy again??

I couldn't imagine it.

Throughout this period of Seemingly Eternal Misery, my closest friends kept saying something to me, over and over, every time I hit the Despair button and wept, again, into my already soaked palms.

It was this:

THINGS WILL GET BETTER. IT'S JUST A QUESTION OF TIME.

To be honest, far from helping me as was intended, it just annoyed me. Not because it sounded condescending, patronising or obvious (it did sound all of those things, and also irritating, frustrating and out of my control) but because I didn't *believe* it. It felt like a hollow lie, just handed out to keep me going.

What the hell was TIME going to do, to repair the nuclear fallout of my life??

Was Time going to bring my happy children back?

Was Time going to step forward and offer me a job with a whacking great pension plan, private health insurance, top childcare incentives and a swivel-chair?

Was Time going to reverse the new grey hairs and deep wrinkles around my eyes?

The whole 'just give it time' thing was one of the most frustrating parts of the split, because I heard it over and over again from people who seemed to be looking a lot less ravaged, exhausted, destroyed and weepy than me, and who, consequently, I quite wanted to punch.

I just wanted the time to have passed already. I wanted it over. I wanted to be through the other side and basking in the new light. I wanted to have healed, to have mended already.

I didn't want to wait for it. I'd waited long enough!

Did I have to wait more?

Yes, I did.

We all have to wait, for healing.

I waited. It took about four years. But the time finally passed, and changed a lot of things for the better.

Time didn't bring back anything we had once had, undo any of the bad times or reverse any of the grey hairs.

But it did heal.

It healed me and healed us all. It gave us the chance to slowly repair the deepest cuts of the break-up, grow protective scabs over them, and let the scars form.

And from that position, it was a lot easier to deal with the millions of other new, unexpected, challenging, emotionally draining, patience-testing, practically difficult, financially painful situations that arose in the years after the split.

So, much as you will want to punch *me* for saying this, if you are currently in the throes of all the fallout, try to give it time.

Hang in there.

Don't do anything rash, or in a state of anger or raw hurt or rage.

Wait for those scabs to form and heal a little.

They offer some protection, and should make things hurt a little less.

Sentimentality Manipulates

All of the above said… beware the softening, editing light of Time.

The fading of deeply hurtful memories, that turn rosy as they become less raw.

The romanticising of the heart-strings.

The deceit of hindsight.

The rewriting of your truth.

If it was bad then, it was bad.

Yes, we can 'laugh at it now'.

We can look back on something fondly, and with less venom and pain.

But when it happened, it was awful. And you were in it.

Don't deny yourself the truth of that.

Recovery and growth can only happen if we deal with hard truth, not edited, cherry-picked highlights.

A Few More Thoughts About Splitting Up

SLAGGING OFF YOUR EX

Don't.

Really, just don't.

Tempting though it is to take all of our sadness, anger, resentment, fear, envy and general aaarrghghghghh about the person we made our kids with and now can't stand the sight of, spin it into an all-decimating fireball of Character Annihilation and light it in front of our children in the hope that they will get on board, throw more petrol on it and hurl it at your ex, while flipping the finger in solidarity...

don't.

Here's what it actually does: far from making them dislike your former partner as much as you do, and thus in some cliquey playground way come and side with you and swap stickers and make a Secret Club that only you guys are members of...

it makes them hate YOU. Much more.

It's brilliant human counter-intuition.

Or rather, it's brilliant, understandable child-loyalty to a parent they still love.

The reason is very simple: THEY are not divorcing your partner. You are.

So keep it that way.

In general, unless one of you has been horrendous and they know it, most children don't want their parents to split up. They also don't want to hate either of you. Or to be made to feel they should.

The person they will hate is the one who says nasty things about the other. Effectively, you're bitching about their friend. And that's not the best way to draw someone towards you, if we're honest.

Basically, anything where the word 'Dad' or 'Mum' is said through gritted teeth, saliva spitting out over your chin in disgust, with the sole intention of conveying maximum dislike, insult, repulsion and sympathy for your situation, is best avoided.

TOP PHRASES I WISH I'D AVOIDED:

Well, if your DAD were actually here to help, then…

If I had a well-paid job, like your Dad…

Luckily for *some people,* they didn't have to give up their whole life to raise their children.

That last one basically means: 'YOU fucked up my whole

life.' Not the most supportive thing to say to a child who is currently more of the opinion that you have just fucked up *their* entire life.

Bottom line is, we all say things in moments of deep emotional pain that we don't mean. Or rather DO mean, but probably should keep to ourselves, a counsellor, a best friend or the bottom of a bottle of wine.

Not our children.

And if you do, as you will, because you're human and we ALL do, always apologise to them afterwards. And mean it.

Admit that you know it was wrong, and you were behaving like a crazed, exhausted, angry banshee. Because, for the most part right now, that's what you are.

And you're sorry. And you'll try not to do it again.

EVERYTHING WE DO DURING A SPLIT INFLUENCES OUR KIDS

How we talk to each other during the tough times.

The decisions we make both during and after it.

Its effect on our health.

Its effect on the whole family.

They watch it all, and take it all in.

And it can, and probably will, have a massive impact on how they go on to have relationships, the way they talk to their partners, and the decisions they make in the future.

I'm not guilt-loading, by the way. We all do things less fabulously than we know we should, or would have liked to, given a little more time and calm, and less OMGMYGOD-WHATISHAPPENING?!

But it's definitely worth being reminded of how much of what WE go through in a split is observed by our children, soaked up by them, and how much we can teach them about doing it better, if it ever comes to it for them.

SPLITTING UP CAN TEACH OUR KIDS LOADS OF GOOD THINGS

About kindness – to their partner and also to themselves.

About honesty.

About admission of fault and taking of blame where it's due.

About apologising.

About forgiveness.

About hard times… and surviving them.

About self-care.

About handling disagreement.

About mental health.

About coping with change.

About resilience.

About cooperation.

About giving.

About self-respect.

About love.

And about hope, always, for a better future.

DON'T MAKE ANY HUGE DECISIONS FOR AT

LEAST A YEAR AFTER SPLITTING UP

I made some very costly mistakes during my split.

I was so crushed by total and utter soul exhaustion, I couldn't do anything else.

I couldn't fight. I didn't want to fight.

I just wanted to sit in a corner and die.

I don't regret it, firstly because there's no point in regret, really, only in learning from our mistakes, and secondly because it was the simplest, quietest and least combative way to do it, at the time.

And anything to reduce further fight and exhaustion, was a good thing.

But I definitely made some decisions that were ill-advised, financially damaging, not entirely necessary, and entirely the result of mental breakdown and burnout.

Had I taken a little more time, waited to feel stronger and more used to the new set-up, had I recovered a little and been more sound of mind, I'd probably have made some different decisions that might have been better, and possibly more 'right' for me, after twenty years of marriage and raising three kids.

So if you can, give it a little time and don't throw the bath out with the dishwater. Or something.

CHERRY-PICKING THE TRUTH

It's easy to decide which side of a story to see.

And when we're hurting, and hurt, it's easiest of all to see only one side.

To curate the memories and decide which ones to keep.

Which version of the truth is truer than the other versions.

Which truth to believe – until what we've decided to believe becomes, to our minds, what actually happened.

It becomes our actual, total truth.

Except it's not.

It's just the truth we've decided to remember.

There's always another truth. Another person's side of the story.

They are allowed it, as much as we are.

Our ex will have his or her own version.

Our children will have theirs.

We might not like them, or agree with them. We might find them hurtful or unfair.

But they are entitled to it, and free to have it.

It is, after all, their truth, as they lived it.

Epilogue

Where Are We All Now?

Well, at the time of writing this, my older children are twenty-two, twenty and sixteen years old.

The eldest has graduated from university, the middle one is in her second year of university now, and their younger brother is starting his A-level years, with big plans to become a billionaire by the age of eighteen. Personally, I'm all for this, as then he can help to pay off all my debts – c'mon lad!

They are healthy, happy, balanced and lovely humans.

As often as diaries and budgets and boyfriend juggles and job interviews allow, they all come stay with us in their holidays and some weekends, and also spend lots of time with their dad, and whoever he is with at the time.

Everyone gets along as well as people ever get along with other people.

Everything is as OK as things can ever be. It's just FINE. No, it's better than fine – it's GOOD! It's taken a lot of work, time, love and occasional hard tongue-biting. But that's families, whatever shape they come in!

They now have a two-year-old sister, whom they adore, and who, it's fair to say, worships them.

I'm engaged to her dad, a kind, beautiful, emotionally intelligent man who has brought me more happiness, laughs and love than I ever thought I'd be capable of experiencing, who has taught me so much about humanity and life, and who once gave me some very valuable advice about letting go, and being happy with what I have.

***

The first round of the Middle Years is nearly over. The bathroom door doesn't slam any more, the sibling rivalries over hair bands and the biscuit tin have been replaced by more adult arguments about politics, life choices and jobs. OK yes, and still the biscuit tin.

I now have the Middle Years Round 2 to look forward to, in about five years from now. GREAT.

But this time, I think I'm more prepared for it.

I've lived through it all before, I know what to expect, what I'll struggle with – and, hopefully, how to deal with it better.

I'm older (and perhaps a *little* wiser), I've learned SO much about life and love, fear and pain, truth and survival in Round 1, all of which I reckon will come in handy.

Most of all, I know what I will miss when it's gone, and how fleeting it all is. When I'm cursing the bedtime stories and the finger-marks on the windows, I'll remember that song I wrote back in Part 1, and know I'll want her to come back, when she's gone.

No, it's not what I ever expected. No, it wasn't any of our plans when we started out in the Very Early Years. No, it sure as HELL wasn't easy, and there are still tricky things to negotiate and weather.

But we are here now, and we are managing.

The Middle Years are some of the strangest, hardest, happiest, most challenging, confusing, tiring and crazy years of our lives.

However they go, and whatever the outcome, we emerge as totally different people from who we were when we went in.

But if we can just go with the flow, be kind, say our thank yous and sorries, learn from our mistakes, let bygones be bygones, appreciate every even semi-bearable moment, put the bins out without resentment, at least try that goddam GCSE maths homework, laugh every day, be grateful for the good things we have while they're still there, face our fears, admit our faults and not be frightened to take a risk sometimes, the Middle Years can pave the way for the best Later Years we could have imagined.

If our teeth can just hold out long enough to enjoy it too.

The End

Acknowledgements

This book will win few awards, but it's a strong contender for the Gold Prize for Slowness.

A large number of people helped to finally see it over the finish line, and in particular I would like to give my huge thanks to:

John Mitchinson, who, many years ago over a coffee – carefully disguised as a gin and tonic – in the extremely elegant Quo Vadis in Soho, listened to my garbled and inelegant waffling about this book idea I'd had about the middle years of parenting, and saw some potential in it;

my wonderful friend Tim Sutton, who gave several hours of his precious time to freeze his nuts off on a cold, windy day in London to film me making my promo video for the book, while I messed it up and swore every five seconds;

my publishers, Unbound, for bearing with me while I didn't deliver a single thing on time, and most especially Xander and Fiona for all their feedback, silent eye-rolling, and immeasurable patience;

my therapist in Venice, who, in my very first session, reminded me that 'you are a writer, Liz, no? You want to finish this book, yes? You will feel good if you finish it, yes? So... write it!' – so I did;

Mike, who relentlessly encouraged me to keep going despite my frequent and I'm sure hugely enjoyable, tear-filled, depressed declarations that I am crap at writing and useless at everything and this is pointless and I give up;

the hundreds of people who wrote to me over the years via social media, email and pigeon post to say they love my writing, were genuinely helped by my books, and WANT me to write this. Some have become friends for life. *All* helped me to keep going;

to all those who pledged to fund the book, and believed in me. I am here, as your faithful book servant, to let you down ungraciously;

and to Harry, for living through the Middle Years with me, and making some of the happiest memories I have. (That holiday in Cornwall was actually lovely. Despite the dog poo.) I know I wasn't the easiest or nicest person to live with at times. Our children are a testament to all the good times – and there were *many*. Thank you.

Patrons

Unbound is the world's first crowdfunding publisher, established in 2011.

We believe that wonderful things can happen when you clear a path for people who share a passion. That's why we've built a platform that brings together readers and authors to crowdfund books they believe in – and give fresh ideas that don't fit the traditional mould the chance they deserve.

This book is in your hands because readers made it possible. Everyone who pledged their support is listed at the front of the book and below. Join them by visiting unbound.com and supporting a book today.

Rachel Andrew
Caroline Archer
Hugh Badini
Steve Bailie
Lydia Baron-Lux
Elizabeth Barrett
Sharon Batty
Rachael Beale

Brian Bilston
Louise Bradford
Angharad Bradley
Laura Brown
Corrina Bryant
Chrissie Bugden
Ali Burns
Xander Cansell
Catherine Cargill
Eva Castillo Aben
Georgina Churchlow
Paula Clark
Ann Clarke
Christopher Clarke
Sacha Cleminson
Jennie Cockcroft
Jonathan Cole
Charlie Connelly
Helen Cooper
Elizabeth Cowburn
John Crawford
Roi Croasdale
Dan Dalton
Michael Danger-Sim
Catherine Dann
Carol Davenport
Catherine Davidson
Kelly Day
Tash Desborough
Les Dodd
Douglas Dougan
Lawrence T Doyle
Rachel Dryden
Eran Edry
Ann Evans
Andy F.R.A.S.E.R.
Ben Falk
Andrew Finch
Livia Firth
Donald and Anna Fraser
Bérénice Froger
Sarah and Andy G
Des Gayle
Jo Gifford
David Gilray
Vicky Gorry
Lesley Halsall
Alice Hart-Davis
Lisa Hayter
Nick Heath
Jane Hemsley-Brown
Victoria Hickman
Jane Hobson
Joanna Hughes
Matt Hulley
Sarah Hunter
Anne Jackson
Bonnie James
Angela Jameson
Julie Jefferies
Alice Jolly
Al Jones
Georgia Kaufmann
Ferris Kawar
Damon Kendrick
Dan Kieran
Laura E. G. Knight
David Landau
Mark Langley
Jane Lawrenson
Anna Lazzaro
Jimmy Leach
Carl Lens
Rory Lindsay
littlepurplegoth
Nikki Livi-Rothwell
Kate Long
Rachael Lucas
Seonaid Mackenzie
Seonaid Mackenzie-Murray
Jo Makin
Ann Maria
Stephen Marsh
David Maxwell-Lyte
Alice May
Penelope McBride
Kerry McCarthy
Claire McClean
Jane Mclaughlin
Toria Megginson

Ben Mills
John Mitchinson
Fiona Mitford
Duncan Moir
Belinda Moore
Mike Morrison
Kirsty Munro
Emma Murphy
Jeremy Musson
Catherine Myhill
Carlo Navato
John New
Celia Nickson
Celia Nickson Bailey
Russell Norman
Kate Oprava
Lucy Owen
Dr. Linda Papadopoulos
Martin Pavlovic
Hector Perez
Helen Perry
Jo Pertwee
Justin Pollard
Donna Potter
Maxine Powell
Sam Preston
Camilla Purdon
Ruth Queen
Jenny Randle
Costantina Rashbrook
A Reader
Judy Reith
Davina Riddle
Ali Rigby
Miranda Robson
Julie Rook
Jaime Rose
Jackie Rosie
Sarah Sandercock
Paul Sandvig
John Schoenbaum
Jenny Seabrook
Helen Sharp
Rosie Sharp
Ben Shephard
Diane Sherratt
Olivia Short
Samina Showghi
Emma Simpson
Christopher Smith
Pen Smith
Paul Spalding
Martin Spencer-Whitton
Sarah Stanbridge
Neil Standring
Cassia Stevens
Katie Stowell
Neil Sutherland
Tim Sutton
Mele Taumoepeau and Ali Knott
Lauren Thomas
Sarah Thomas
Bill Thompson
Kelly Titley
Paul Tompsett
Amanda Towers
Camilla Tress
Charlotte Tubb
Erica Tyler-Chamberlain
Julia Walker
Michaela Walker
Charlotte Walton
Selina Ware
Emma Webb
Michael Welton
Sophia Wickham
Sandy Wilkie
Rhodes Williams
Derek Wilson
Pam Wilson
Rob Wiltsher
Richard Wood
Ivan Woods
Stacey Woods
Nick Wray
Alison Wright
Kate Young
Anne & Thorsten Zwieback